I0648857

Mr. (Edward) Jerningham

**The Welch Heiress**

A Comedy

Mr. (Edward) Jerningham

**The Welch Heiress**
*A Comedy*

ISBN/EAN: 9783744661973

Printed in Europe, USA, Canada, Australia, Japan

Cover: Foto ©Thomas Meinert / pixelio.de

More available books at **www.hansebooks.com**

THE

# WELCH HEIRESS,

A

*COMEDY.*

THE SECOND·EDITION.

1795.

# EARL OF HARCOURT.

As I have attempted to write a Comedy at the flattering inftigation of your Lordfhip, the following fcenes have a natural claim to your protection. If, when you prompted and encouraged me to court the Comic Mufe, you had imparted to me at the fame time fome fhare of your inftinctive penetration into character--- of your elegant, but impreffive ridicule of fafhionable levities---had you configned to my hand the clue that guides you in the chace and detection of folly through the intricate windings of her labyrinth, I fhould have prefented to you a Comedy more worthy of your attention. Such as it is, it offers me an opportunity of publickly acknowledging the high value I fet upon a friendfhip, which I have had the happinefs of enjoying fo many years.

I have the honor to be,

Your moft obedient

Humble Servant,

EDWARD JERNINGHAM.

# *PROLOGUE*

# WELCH HEIRESS.

WRITTEN BY JOHN TAYLOR, ESQ.

*Spoken by Mr. Barrymore.*

---

" SHOOT Folly as it flies." Such is the game,
At which, 'tis faid, the Comic Mufe fhould aim;
The darker paffions that the heart deform,
And fpread o'er groaning ftates the moral ftorm,
Are pompous themes the fportive Maid refigns,
To fwell her folemn Sifter's lofty lines.
Yet when fhe fain would ftrike fuch tow'ring prey,
The ferious Damfel takes the fafeft way;
Tho' proud yet prudent---wounding guilt too high,
To wake in you the felf-reproaching figh;
In fluggifh apathy you carelefs fit,
Nor fmart for crimes that you could ne'er commit:
But, in the comic province, who fhall dare
To touch the faults that you may haply fhare?
For confcience then may ftrengthen the appeal,
And bid you crufh what forces her to feel.

For Virtue, zealous and difdaining awe,
E'en fear'd by thofe too mighty for the law,
The Stage, through ev'ry ftation, Vice has try'd,
And honeft Satire has her lafh applied.

Hence,

Hence, while the Comic Mufe muft fear to wound,
She ftill is doom'd to courfe o'er beaten ground;
Again bring forward what too well you know,·
Or, if a novelty, fome monfter fhew.

   To-night our Bard, who long has ftruck the lyre,
A modeft minftrel of the plaintive choir,
Attempts for once a harmlefs laugh to raife,
More dreading cenfure than prefuming praife.
One point we fairly in his caufe may plead---
For know, he dares to touch the fcribbling breed;
Dares ftrip from dull conceit its bold pretence,
And prove an Author may be void of fenfe.
Then let your candour countenance the grace
That freely owns the follies of his race;
And fure our Bard e'en Malice need not fear,
(Could Malice lurk in fpecious ambufh *here*)
E'en fhe may yield her pittance of applaufe
To him whofe vent'rous pen a brother draws;
For while thus fportive on a fcribbling elf,
Our fimple Poet may deride himfelf.

The

*The following Lines, written by the Rev. Mr.*
*PRITCHARD, Jun. before he knew the*
*Author was in poſſeſſion of another Pro-*
*logue, contain too much Merit to be ſup-*
*preſſed.*

THERE liv'd at Argos once a youth of fame,
(So Horace tells) and Lycas was his name,
Who, (if there is a joy which mad men know,
And ſuch as madneſs only can beſtow)
By the ſtrong force of its prevailing pow'r,
Wak'd to freſh tranſport ev'ry new-born hour.
Each viſionary ſcene that fancy drew,
His mind embodied, and confirm'd it true.
Oft, in the height of his diſtemper's rage,
He ſaw, or fancy'd that he ſaw, a ſtage;
Where as he heard the ſelf-imagin'd ſound,
And trod, or thought he trod, dramatic ground;
Where, with nice ſkill in imitative art,
Each ſon of Theſpis ſeem'd to play his part,
The fond conceit drew down his loud applauſe,
As tho' reality had been the cauſe,
And ev'ry member, head, hands, lips, and eyes,
Profeſs'd their praiſe, and teſtified ſurprize.

If ſuch the charm where fancy gave delight,
Let truth, not fiction, plead our cauſe to-night;
And,

And, as I come to take a nearer view,
Pleading for him who ftrives to pleafure you,
Oh! may propitious Beauty* fmile reward!
May Science † favour, and the Gods ‡ regard!

Sons of renown, the bards of ancient days,
Wore on their heads a circling crown of bays,
Thefe bloom eternal, for to them belong
The grace, the pride, the energies of fong;
The tale well-told, the animated line,
The glow of fentiment, and thought divine;
Yet ftill there bloffoms many a virgin flow'r,
On the fair fpot where Genius rears her bow'r;
Of thefe our bard prefents before your view,
One of a fimple, but unfully'd hue;
Should the mild off'ring kind acceptance fhare,
Tis your's to weave the crown, and his to wear.

---

* To the Boxes.　　† To the Pit.　　‡ To the Galleries.

# CHARACTERS.

| | |
|---|---|
| Lord MELCOURT | Mr. Palmer. |
| Mr. FASHION     - | Mr. Barrymore. |
| Sir PEPPER PLIN- LIMMON } | Mr. Dodd. |
| Mr. PHRENSY   - | Mr. Bannister, Jun. |
| Mr. FANCY   ⌐   - | Mr. R. Palmer, |
| | |
| Lady BELLAIR   - | Miss Farren. |
| Lady PLINLIMMON | Miss Pope. |
| Miss PLINLIMMON | Mrs. Jordan. |

---

SCENE---Melcourt-Hall, near Town.

# WELCH HEIRESS,

## *A COMEDY.*

---

## ACT I.

*Enter Lady* BELLAIR---*Mr.* FASHION.

*Mr.* FASHION.

I AM happy at your Ladyſhip's arrival. We expected you laſt night.

*Lady Bellair.* I purpoſely avoided coming laſt
night, that I might not be complicated in the em-
barraſſment of the Welch family's arrival, whom
I underſtand came yeſterday. What ſort of creatures are they? How many did the caravan conſiſt
of? I expect to ſee the whole race of Shenkin.

*Mr. Faſh.* Do not be alarmed as to their num-
ber; I will give your Ladyſhip a liſt of the *dra-
matis perſonæ,* and a faint ſketch of their characters.

*Lady B.* Pray do! for I have ſeen nobody, not
even my brother, the *padrone della caſa.*

*Mr. Faſh.* Lord Melcourt, I know, is walked
out; I was juſt enquiring after him. But to return
to the ſubject;---Yeſterday evening, the family
coach, covered with duſt, and much damaged by
the toil and length of the journey, waddled up to

the

the hall-door in great labour, and was happily delivered of Sir Pepper Plinlimmon, Lady Plinlimmon, Miſs Plinlimmon, and a *femme de chambre*; two ſervants attended on Welch ponies. The coach, I muſt inform you, contained originally five perſons, but it miſcarried on the road of Mr. Taffey, their chaplain, who could not bear the inſide of a carriage. He is, however, expected to-morrow, in the baſket of ſome ſtage-coach.

*Lady B.* I fancy we ſhall be able to do without Mr. Taffey.

*Mr. Faſh.* Indeed you are miſtaken. He is one of the eſſential perſonages in our drama, for he is to join the hands of Lord Melcourt and Miſs Plinlimmon.

*Lady B.* What ſort of a thing is the girl?

*Mr. Faſh.* She is very well as to beauty; her ſhape elegantly and harmoniouſly formed, but when in motion, ungraceful. Her mind is a compound of ignorance and information, like the waving branches that give a checquered kind of light. She made us laugh laſt night at ſupper with the childiſh ſimplicity of her queſtions, and ſometimes ſhe excited our admiration at the quickneſs of her repartee, and the ſolidity of her judgment; in a word, ſhe appears to be an inſpired ideot.

*Lady B.* Now let me have the portrait of Sir Pepper.

*Mr. Faſh.* Sir Pepper is a plain, unaſſuming man, ſubject at times to a warmth of temper, and whoſe local train of impoveriſhed ideas are quite unſuitable to the ſcene he is now entering upon, and to the company with which he is now to aſſociate. His mind has received a peculiar biaſs reſpecting the prophecies that have been floating of late, and he is almoſt convinced the world will be at an end before his daughter has brought Lord Melcourt a ſon and heir.

*Lady*

*Lady B.* I confefs, I like the whimficallity of that notion ; it will ferve to amufe us.

*Mr. Fafh.* As for Lady Plinlimmon, fhe has a confiderable fhare of vanity; half of which fhe fpends in admiration of her daughter-in-law, the other fhe confumes upon herfelf. She imagines fhe has a refined tafte for literature, that fhe is a fupreme judge of painting, and---

*Lady B.* Oh ! then fhe is intolerable.

*Mr. Fafh.* By no means. There is a broad good-humour about her which makes her inoffenfive. She looks with impatience for the honour of ce-menting an acquaintance with your Ladyfhip.

*Lady B.* I think, from your defcription, it will not be unentertaining to pafs a day or two with thefe Welch Emigrants. But does my brother feem happy at his approaching nuptials ?

*Mr. Fafh.* Yefterday he feemed at firft over-come by the invafion of thefe Vandals; but his native mirth rallied, and at the clofe of the evening he was himfelf again. But here he comes.

### Enter Lord MELCOURT.

*Lord Mel.* Sifter, you are welcome ! You look in high beauty. The elegant circles in town will be eclipfed without you. Have you feen our new kindred?

*Lady B.* Not yet. Mr. Fafhion has been giv-ing me a flight fketch of them.

*Lord Mel.* Well, I am ready to confign Sir Pepper, and Lady Plinlimmon to the full dif-charge of your raillery; but fpare, I intreat you, my fhepherdefs of the Alps.

*Lady B.* Never fear; never fear.

*Lord Mel.* Lady Plinlimmon looks for your arrival with all the flutter of anxious expectation. Your fame, like an artful prologue, has fmoothed

the

the way to a kind reception : fhe talks of you as the paragon of excellence ; fhe will ftudy your whole perfon; obferve every motion, attitude, and every article of your drefs.

*Mr. Fafh.* Lady Bellair may be faid to be a capital picture from the gallery of fafhion, for Lady Plinlimmon to copy.

*Lady B.* I will venture to fay, without the impeachment of vanity, that the copy will not come up to the merit of the original.

*Mr. Fafh.* Your Ladyfhip is perfectly right.

*Lady B.* But tell me, brother, don't you feel, independent of the charms of your young bride, an uncommon elafticity of mind in the removal of the incumbrances which this marriage will effect ?

*Lord Mel.* Yes. Upon that ground I plant the ftandard of my gaudieft ftreamer. I have had a private conference with Sir Pepper, and his immediate relinquifhing of his Brecknockfhire eftate will enable me to part with my Irifh acres, and fatisfy all my noify claimants; who, like a voracious pack of hounds, have chaced me from hill to dale, and notwithftanding the windings of excufes, and the intricate mazes of delay, would have foon overtaken me, had not this golden fhower from the Welch mountains put an end to the chace.

*Lady B.* Bravo! Are we to expect any more company ?

*Lord Mel.* I have invited my friend Fancy, the miniature-painter. I expect alfo Phrenfy, the poet, whom you have often heard me talk of; he will fuit Lady Plinlimmon, and their mutual eccentricities will divert us.

*Mr. Fafh.* I am glad that oddity will be added to the group; you have frequently amufed me with anecdotes concerning him. When will he be here ?

*Lord Mel.* I expect him every minute. He writes word he will be here to-day, but begs his
coming

coming may be a fecret; and, as he is not perfonnally known to any body but myfelf, he defires to affume the name of Tombftone.

*Mr. Fafh.* What a whim! What can he mean?

*Lord M.* Moft likely he is afraid of his creditors---however, do not betray him to the reft of our fociety. But here come our Welch relatives, (*Enter Sir* PEPPER PLINLIMMON, *Lady* PLINLIMMON, *and Mifs* PLINLIMMON.) Give me leave to prefent Lady Bellair, to your Ladyfhip.

*Lady Plin.* Independent of the connection that is taking place between our families, I rejoice at the opportunity that now ·offers of commencing an acquaintance with Lady Bellair.

*Lady B.* Your Ladyfhip does me a great deal of honour. I hope Sir Pepper, you will like this part of the world fufficiently to engage you to ftay among us fome time.

*Lady Plin.* What eafe! What elegance! (*Afide.*

*Sir P. Plin.* I fhould wifh to enjoy your Ladyfhip's fociety, but I am rather difpofed to return as foon as I can; for if, as Noftradamus fays, we are in the fifth act I fhould like to be at home when the curtain drops.

*Lady Plin.* Dear Sir Pepper, do not cloud the fplendour of Lady Bellair's mind, with the dark mifts of your odious prophecies.

*Lady B.* I beg your Ladyfhip will let Sir Pepper fay what he choofes, I am not eafily alarmed: credulity is not my foible. But this is a converfation of too fevere a caft for our young bride:· you, my dear, may fend your expecting eye through a long and gay perfpective.

*Mifs P.* So I do! I expect to have fine cloaths, to go to a great many balls, and I expect to be married!

*Sir P. Plin.* Your Ladyfhip will exufe the wild fimplicity of my daughter.

*Lady B.*

*Lady B.* Oh! I am a great admirer of artleſs ſimplicity; it is as rare to be met with as ſincerity.

*Lady Plin.* When ſhe has exchanged the rude breezes of the mountain where ſhe was bred, for the gentler gales of poliſhed ſociety, ſhe will aſſimi- late with the ſoft elegance of her new ſituation.

*Mr. Faſh.* Lady Bellair herſelf could not have invented a metaphor more happily alluſive.

*Sir P. Plin.* My wife is very metaphori*call.*

*Miſs Plin.* Yes! we all have our different *calls*; mamma is metaphori*call*---papa is propheti*call*--- I am comi*call*---the old curate, near Plinlimmon Caſtle, is claſſi*call*, and his wife is dropſi*call!*

*Lady Plin.* You muſt check this careleſs volu- bility.

*Lord Mel.* Suppoſe, gentlemen, we leave the ladies to confer by themſelves. Will you allow me, Sir Pepper, to ſhew you the Vandyke I men- tioned laſt night?

*Sir P. Plin.* If you pleaſe.

(*Exeunt Sir* PEPPER, *Mr.* FASHION, *Lord* MELCOURT.

*Lady Plin.* I ſhould wiſh your Ladyſhip not to be impreſſed with an idea that my daughter-in- law is deficient in the great outline of education, though ſhe has not yet received the laſt touchings of embelliſhment. I myſelf have been her tuto- reſs, and have read to her ſeveral of the beſt En- gliſh authors.

*Miſs Plin.* And all the Welch poets.

*Lady B.* I am perſuaded Miſs Plinlimmon is deficient in nothing that is abſolutely requiſite for the ſtation ſhe is going to aſcend: as for thoſe de- licate finiſhings, that faſhionable elegance de- mands---

*Lady Plin.* Your Ladyſhip's ſociety will ſupply. I conſign this young Alpine plant to your care: 'tis yours to give the pliant branches their proper direction, and to breathe on them a playful air of eaſy negligence. With your permiſſion, I will now
with-

withdraw for the purpofe of my girls imbibing from your Ladyſhip thoſe nameleſs graces you only can beſtow. (*Exit Lady* PLINLIMMON.

*Miſs Plin.* What are thoſe things mamma ſays you are to beſtow upon me?

*Lady B.* My friendſhip! And you in return muſt have ſome friendſhip for me, and ſpeak to me with confidence upon every point that relates to your marriage with my brother. By what he has ſaid to me, I find he is extremely attached to you: I hope his attachment will meet with an equal return on your part.

*Miſs Plin.* That is as it may be.

*Lady B.* I am ſure Lord Melcourt is reckoned by all the ladies very handſome, amiable, enter-taining, and ---

*Miſs Plin.* I know all that, and I ſhould be very partial to him, if ---

*Lady B.* If what, my dear?

*Miſs Plin.* If ---

*Lady B.* Has he done any thing to offend you?

*Miſs Plin.* No! but he has done nothing to pleaſe me.

*Lady B.* Does he appear to neglect you? I re-collect he was uncommonly aſſiduous in writing to you laſt winter.

*Miſs Plin.* Oh yes! he frequently wrote to me, and he uſed to ſay in his letters, that when I ſhould come to Melcourt Hall, we ſhould wander through the groves together, and he would ſay ſuch tender things to me by the river-ſide. Now we were by the river-ſide yeſterday evening, and ſcarce one word did he ſay to me, but converſed with my papa about the winding of his river; egad! I wiſh it was wound round his neck.

*Lady B.* Fie, child! You muſt not imagine that Lord Melcourt's attention is to be totally devoted to you.

*Miſs*

*Miſs Plin.* Am I then not to expect any ſhare of his converſation? Is there to be no time for wooing? no flirtation? no whiſpering? no toying? no innocent anticipation?

*Lady B.* Miſs Plinlimmon, the manufacturing of love in Wales may perhaps be as coarſe as a ſackcloth, but in this part of the world, the cupids of faſhion weave the fine texture with a light and inviſible hand.

*Miſs Plin.* Inviſible indeed! But if I am never to partake of his company, what am I come here for? what ſhall I be the better for being married to him? where is the advantage?

*Lady B.* You will obtain the advantage of his name and title; you will move in a higher ſphere.

*Miſs Plin.* But I always underſtood, that wedlock was a kind of travelling through life together?

*Lady B.* So it is, but then it is like travelling in the double ſtage-coach; you go the ſame journey together, without ſeeing or incommoding one another.

*Miſs Plin.* I hate the double ſtage-coach; I like a vis-a-vis much better. However, if Lord Melcourt does not become more aſſiduous, he may be ſupplanted---Faſhion is much more attentive.

*Enter Lord* MELCOURT.

*Lord Mel.* I aſk pardon for interrupting you; but the odd character I ſpoke of is arrived; he begs to ſee me in private; he is now coming.

*Lady B.* We will retire immediately.

*(Exeunt Lady* BELLAIR *and Miſs* PLINLIMMON.

*Enter*

*Enter fervant---announces Mr.* TOMBSTONE.---
*Enter Mr.* PHRENSY.

*Mr. Phrenfy.* Your fervant---I am obliged to you for your invitation---I have an epithalamium for the occafion; fhall I read it?

*Lord Mel.* All in good time: tell me firft why you affume another name?

*Mr. Phrenfy.* You fhall hear, but do not betray me.

*Lord Mel.* You may rely upon me.

*Mr. Phrenfy.* Shall not I read the epithalamium firft?

*Lord Mel.* No, no! I am impatient for your hiftory?

*Mr. Phrenfy.* Well, you fhall hear it---but I am certain you will be pleafed with the epithalamium.

*Lord Mel.* I have no doubt, but let me know the fecret motive of your changing your name, before we are interrupted.

*Mr. Phrenfy.* Do you think your fervants will know me?

*Lord Mel.* I have an entire new fet.

*Mr. Phrenfy.* That makes me happy.

*Lord Mel.* Was it the fear of your creditors?

*Mr. Phrenfy.* No fuch terreftrial motive urged me to affume another name: this liberty I have taken with myfelf flows from a more fublime caufe, than the apprehenfion of bailiffs! I will now difclofe the myftery---unlefs you choofe to hear the epithalamium firft---

*Lord Mel.* Do not trifle any longer, but let me know the purport of this myfterious conduct.

*Mr. Phrenfy.* Envy, which attends living authors, has purfued me with great implacability.

*Lord Mel.* I do not recollect that I ever heard your works cenfured.

*Mr. Phrenfy.* Likely enough---cenfure would have excited notice---notice would have led to obfervation---obfervation to juftice---juftice to admiration---no no! Envy, my Lord took another method with me, fhe fome how or other, contrived to breathe over me and my works a dread repofe. The warehoufe where my productions are depofited, refembles a family vault where all my numerous progeny are at reft! And are only diftinguifhed from one another by labels---fuch as Phrenfy's comedies--Phrenfy's tragedies--Phrenfy's fatires---Phrenfy's ---

*Lord Mel.* But what has all this to do with the changing of your name?

*Mr. Phrenfy.* I am now coming to the mark: my friends have foothed me with the idea, that pofterity will do me juftice---that pofterity will fay to thefe fleepers, arife! Then will my comedies, my tragedies, my odes, fhake off their duft and dazzle the admiring world.

*Lord Mel.* What is all this to the purpofe?

*Mr. Phrenfy.* You fhall hear---inftead of patiently waiting the natural procefs of time, I conceived a ftratagem of anticipating my triumphs, and of taking a fhort cut to pofterity.

*Lord Mel.* How do you mean---by cutting your throat?

*Mr. Phrenfy.* 'Tis done, 'tis done---

*Lord Mel.* What's done?

*Mr. Phrenfy.* I have killed myfelf; that is to fay I have given out that I am dead. This is the reafon for changing my name---envy was never played fuch a trick before---

*Lord Mel.* But why take the melancholy name of Tombftone?

*Mr. Phrenfy.* That is to keep me in recollection that I am dead.

*Lord*

*Lord Mel.* There is fenfe in that.

*Mr. Phrenfy.* But this ftratagem, my Lord, has not yet anfwered my fanguine expectation.

*Lord Mel.* How fo?

*Mr. Phrenfy.* I have been three weeks dead, and would you believe that there has not been in any of the papers, an elegy, a pofthumous puff, or a line'in my commendation.

*Lord Mel.* That is very ftrange.

*Mr. Phrenfy.* Egad! A tallow-chandler might have flipt out of the world, as eafily as I have done.

*Lord Mel.* How did you infert your death in the papers, for it efcaped my notice.

*Mr. Phrenfy.* Simply thus---yefterday died, univerfally lamented, the eminent poet, Claffical Phrenfy, Efq.

*Lord Mel.* To be fure, nothing could be more fimple and modeft---but I have an idea, that I think will ferve your fcheme better---I will have it inferted in the papers, and you fhall draw up the paragragh, to this purpofe---yefterday the eminent poet, Claffical Phrenfy, Efq. died fuddenly, at Melcourt-Hall, where he was upon a vifit to his friend, Lord Melcourt.

*Mr. Phrenfy.* Very good---excellent conception.

*Lord Mel.* The circumftance of making your exit at my country-houfe, during the interefting moment of my nuptials, will give your death an eclat.

*Mr. Phrenfy.* This fecond edition of my death, with additions, will do admirably faith, but what will your company fay, when they fhall read the paragraph?

*Lord Mel.* I fhall take particular care, that none of them fhall fee it.

*Mr.*

*Mr. Phrenfy.* But what does your Lordſhip ſmile at?

*Lord Mel.* Another idea occurs, which will ſerve to enrich the paragraph---

*Mr. Phrenfy.* As how?

*Lord Mel.* Fancy, the miniature-painter, will be here to day---I ſhall tell him as a profound ſecret that you lie dead in the houſe, and that it is unknown to the company---and I will beg of him, as you are my friend, to take a faint ſketch of you---

*Mr. Phrenfy.* This will, as your Lordſhip ſays, enrich the paragraph, which may run thus---Mr. Phrenfy being the intimate friend of Lord Melcourt, an eminent painter from town was ſent for, to take a likeneſs of the great poet.

*Lord Mel.* Admirable! You have only to whiten your face, and make yourſelf like a ghoſt in an opera, the painter ſhall only peep at you, and then finiſh the ſketch from memory---truſt to my contrivance, you ſhall not be detected.

*Mr. Phrenfy.* I will go and prepare the paragraph. (*Phrenfy going, returns*) your Lordſhip then does not wiſh to hear the epithalamium firſt?

*Lord Mel.* No, no! I expect the painter every minute. (*Exit Mr.* PHRENSY.) Self conceit--- good humour---with abſurdity, are happily blend-ed in that man's compoſition.

*Enter* SERVANT.

*Servant.* Mr. Fancy is arrived---
*Lord Mel.* Bid him come in---

*Enter*

*Enter Mr.* Fancy.

*Mr. Fancy.* I wifh your Lordfhip joy, I flatter myfelf you have not fent for me, to be an idle fpectator---I hope I fhall have the honor of draw-·ing the bride.

*Lord Mel.* Moft affuredly---the art fuffers when you are idle.

*Mr. Fancy.* Have you affembled many of your friends upon this occafion?

*Lord Mel.* No---Lady Bellair is come, and Mr. Fafhion, and a literary acquaintance of mine, Mr. Tombftone.

*Mr. Fancy.* I never heard of his name.

*Lord Mel.* He has lived a great deal abroad, he is lately returned from Africa; I had another ingenious man here, and he was my particular friend, but a fudden death has deprived me of that invaluable perfon: what I am going to relate, is a fecret, nobody is acquainted with the terrible accident, except a confidential fervant. Poor Phrenfy, the poet, died fuddenly laft night; he is now in the houfe, and is to be removed this even-ing: I fhould be happy to have a refemblance of my old friend, and if you would have the good-nefs to take a hafty fketch of him, you would in-finitely oblige me.

*Mr. Fancy.* I can have no objection.

*Lord Mel.* Let all this tranfaction be as fecret as the grave.

*Mr. Fancy.* You may depend upon me.

*Enter Mr.* Phrensy, *with a paper.*

*Mr. Phrenfy.* Here is the paragraph for your infpection.

*Lord*

*Lord Mel.* (*taking the paper*) I ſhall look at it another time. Let me have the ſatisfaction of introducing two gentlemen to one another, who are formed for each other's acquaintance; Mr. Tombſtone, let me preſent you to Mr. Fancy. I muſt now beg permiſſion to leave you together; I ſhall return in a few moments. (*Exit Lord* MELCOURT.

*Mr. Fancy.* I am happy in commencing an acquaintance with ſo ingenious a gentleman.     I ſhould be proud to draw your portrait.

*Mr. Phrenſy.* (*Smiling*) You ſhall, Mr. Fancy. I ſuppoſe the bride is to be embelliſhed by your pencil?

*Mr. Fancy.* Of courſe. But Lord Melcourt did not ſend for me merely to paint the young lady.

*Mr. Phrenſy.* Your pencil will undoubtedly run through the whole family.

*Mr. Fancy.* Likely enough. But I have another meaning. I am ſent for---I am ſure Mr. Tombſtone may be truſted; and as the firſt fruits of my friendſhip for you, I will depoſit in your breaſt a profound ſecret.

*Mr. Phrenſy.* I will in return communicate to you, the firſt ſecret that is whiſpered in my ear.

*Mr. Fancy.* I have, then, to inform you, that there is a perſon lies dead in the houſe, and Lord Melcourt has begged I would juſt catch a reſemblance of his departed friend.

*Mr. Phrenſy.* Who is it?

*Mr. Fancy.* Phrenſy, the poet!

*Mr. Phrenſy.* Indeed! Is that great and unrivalled man no more?

*Mr. Fancy.* You are too magnificent in the epithets you apply to Mr. Phrenſy.

*Mr. Phrenſy.* By no means! Reflect what an awful taſk is now impoſed upon you! Methinks I

ſee

fee you advance, with fublime emotion, towards the honoured couch that bears the breathlefs image of that immortal man!

*Mr. Fancy.* But whence this enthufiafm? After all it muft be confeffed, that the friendfhip of Lord Melcourt was the higheft feather in his cap.

*Mr. Phrenfy.* Talk not to me of feather, or of cap! His head was encircled with laurel, wove by the public hand! For fhame Mr. Fancy, is it thus you revere the illuftrious dead?

*Mr. Fancy.* Don't be fo warm, Mr. Tomb-ftone, I am perhaps a little ungenerous in fpeaking againft the dead who cannot defend themfelves: but tell me difpaffionately, do you admire poor Phrenfy's writings?

*Mr. Phrenfy.* I do! I know them by heart, have you a mind to hear the fixteenth fcene of his tragi-comedy, in fix acts, where the princefs catches her.---

*Mr. Fancy.* No, no! I will not give you the trouble of repeating your friend's verfes.

*Mr. Phrenfy.* My friend's verfes! you fay right, yes my intimate friend; he never wrote a line without confulting me.

*Mr. Fancy.* But if he was fo dear a friend, how comes it you are not more affected by his death?

*Mr. Phrenfy.* I am aftonifhed, ftunned, bewildered at the dreadful fecret you difclofed! When the firft impreffion is fubfided, grief will fucceed: Lord Melcourt out of affection for me fecreted the melancholy event, but I begin to feel myfelf overpowered. (*goes afide with his handkerchief to his eyes.*

*Enter Lord* MELCOURT.

*Lord Mel.* What is the matter with Mr. Tomb-ftone?

*Mr:*

*Mr. Fancy.* Inadvertantly I informed him of the death of Mr. Phrenfy, not knowing the intimacy that fubfifted between them.

*Lord Mel.* How could you be fo imprudent? (*goes up to Mr. Phrenfy*) Dear Tombftone, do not yield to this inordinate affliction.

*Mr. Phrenfy.* How can I command my grief? (*throws his arms round Lord Melcourt's neck.*)

*Lord Mel.* I take no inconfiderable fhare in your diftrefs.

*Mr. Phrenfy.* Undoubtedly you do, in loofing Mr. Phrenfy, you lofe your panegyrift---think how often he has regaled your Lordfhip with the thickeft cream of dedication.

*Lord Mel.* Forbear to remind me, you affect me too much.

*Mr. Fancy.* What a fituation I am in! I thought I was invited to the abode of feftivity, inftead of which, I am come into the houfe of mourning; I had better return to town.

*Lord Mel.* By no means! When this mutual fympathetic emotion is over, we fhall return to our former mirth.

*Mr Fancy.* Your Lordfhip appeared very eafy and jocund juft now.

*Lord Mel.* You then faw me during the intervals of the firft and fecond paroxifm of grief.

*Mr. Fancy.* Is then your Lordfhip's affliction methodifed into acts like a play, with paufes between the divifions.

*Lord Mel.* Indeed Mr. Fancy, this is not a moment for raillery, let me entreat you to leave us, we fhall be more compofed prefently.

*Mr. Fancy.* Well, I will obey your commands!
(*Exit.*

Lord MELCOURT *and Mr.* PHRENSY *burft into laughing.*

*Lord*

*Lord Mel.* We fhall have ftill more entertainment with the painter, when he has drawn your
picture.

*Mr. Phrenfy.* I am impatient for that fcene, I
will go and prepare myfelf.

*Lord Mel.* My valet de chambre, who has my
inftructions, and who is in our confidence will
affift and furnifh you with whatever is neceffary
for the purpofe, I muft now join the company.

**END OF THE FIRST ACT.**

D         A C T II.

# ACT II.

*Lord* MELCOURT---*Mr.* FANCY, *with a pallet in his hand---a couch at some distance, on which Mr.* PHRENSY *lies, disguised as dead.*

*Lord Mel.* Shall we now approach the venerable remains of the great man.

*Mr. Fancy.* Give me leave to mingle my colours a little.

*Lord Mel.* I am afraid the task I have imposed upon you, is unpleasant: you feel, I make no doubt, very disagreeable sensations upon this occasion.

*Mr. Fancy.* Not in the least, a lifeless frame does not impress me with any disturbance; I drew Lady Fidget's dead monkey the other day without any kind of perturbation.

*Lord Mel.* But, Mr. Fancy, do you make no distinction between Lady Fidget's dead monkey, and the remains of my friend?

*Mr. Fancy.* As he was your friend, I respect him, but does your Lordship really think he is worthy of those encomiums, that you and Mr. Tombstone, so profusely bestowed upon him?

*Lord Mel.* My partiality may perhaps cast a little suffusion over my judgment. But tell me, do
you

you not venerate his memory? Do you not admire his works?

*Mr. Fancy.* Perhaps as much as your Lordſhip, 'tis impoſſible with ſo refined an underſtanding as yours to receive any entertainment from his writings; the characters in his plays, for example, may be compared to the incongruities that we meet with on ſign-poſts: things that never exiſted in nature, ſuch as blue boars, black ſwans, dragons, and mermaids---I never felt a more pleaſing invitation to a ſlumber, than I did at his laſt comedy, which unfortunately I did not enjoy long, for I was rouſed by a thouſand cat-calls.

(*Mr.* PHRENSY *ſtarts up from the couch.*)

*Mr Phrenſy.* 'Tis falſe, 'tis falſe, no cat-call was heard at my comedy, though I am dead, I am not damned---

*Mr. Fancy.* (*Recovering from his fright*) I perceive it was a trick.

*Mr. Phrenſy.* Trick or no trick, my works will live when the memory of Lady Fidget, her monkey and yourſelf, will be ſwept from the face of the earth---baſe calumniator---

*Lord Mel.* I beg I may be the negociator of peace between the living and the dead; in the firſt place I can aſſure Mr. Fancy no indignity was meant to him---Mr. Phrenſy, for particular reaſons, having given out that he was dead, I thought a portrait of the author, by a celebrated painter, would add luſtre to the poſthumous edition of his works.

*Mr. Fancy.* Then I forgive him.　(*Runs to embrace him.*)

*Mr. Phrenſy.* But tell me firſt, how can I forgive the ſcurrilous obſervations you ſo liberally beſtowed upon my compoſitions?

*Lord Mel.* Dear Phrenfy, you do not imagine that the painter was in earneſt---flatter him a little                              (*aſide to Fancy.*

*Mr. Fancy.* I hope I am not ſo deſtitute of taſte. So far from ſleeping at your comedy, I diſturbed the boxes with my peals of laughter.

*Mr Phrenfy.* Give me your hand.

*Mr. Fancy.* Then the parts were ſo chequered with ſentimental and pathetic paſſages.

*Mr. Phrenfy.* Excuſe me, there was nothing pathetic in my comedy, nor any thing like ſentiment.

*Mr. Fancy.* I only mean in the winding up of your comedy, where the butcher's daughter kneels.

*Mr. Phrenfy.* My dear Sir, you are ſpeaking of my tragedy.

*Lord Mel.* Phrenfy, you muſt excuſe him--- Fancy's mind has not yet recovered from the confuſion, your ſudden burſting from the dead occaſioned! You had better retire and relapſe into Tombſtone.

*Mr. Phrenfy.* I will follow your direction--- and as you, Mr. Fancy, are acquainted with my ſecret hiſtory---let us for the future be friends.
                              (*Exit Mr.* PHRENSY.

*Mr. Fancy.* Now we are alone---I muſt declare you was rather too hard upon me, in expoſing me as you did to the indignation of the enraged poet---

*Lord Mel.* I only intended a little innocent ſport, I did not think he would have ruſhed upon us ſo rudely, it was his irritability in hearing himſelf abuſed, that made him riſe from the dead.

*Mr. Fancy.* Then it was my own doing, for the abuſe was all mine: I muſt now prepare to draw the living; the ladies I believe, are now waiting for me.

*Lord*

*Lord Mel.* I will follow you---

(*Exit Mr.* FANCY.


*Enter Mr.* FASHION.

*Lord Mel.* I wiſh, Faſhion, you had been here
ſometime ago---we had an excellent ſcene between the painter and the dead poet---the painter
was almoſt in an hyſteric.

*Mr. Faſhion.* I think theſe two characters will
afford us ſtill more entertainment.

*Lord Mel.* I hope ſo---for I want ſomething to
draw off my attention, and to prevent me from
fixing too ſteady an eye upon this bride of mine,
I ſhall be aſhamed to introduce her among my
acquaintance next winter.

*Mr. Faſh.* Do not be under any apprehenſion,
the inſtructions of Lady Bellair, Mrs. Townlife,
and Lady Angelica Worthleſs, will refine the rude
ſimplicity of your wild mountain-girl.

*Lord Mel.* Though I have a high opinion of
thoſe able modern profeſſors, I am inclined to
think this Welch girl will baffle all their ſkill,
ſhe will never through them, as through filtering
ſtones, diveſt herſelf of the heterogeneous matter,
the heavy particles, the nauſeous lees ſhe has im-
bibed from her country education, from the manners of Sir Pepper, and from the vulgarity of the
mother-in-law---no, no, 'tis impoſſible---

*Mr. Faſh.* I aſk your pardon---when ſhe has
been decanted off into poliſhed ſociety ſhe will
leave the dregs behind.

*Lord Mel.* I wiſh it may be ſo---I muſt now
look for the painter, who is going to draw the
portrait of my bride elect.

*Mr. Faſh.* I will not detain you.

(*Exeunt*

SCENE.

Scene---*The Saloon. Lady Plinlimmon, Mifs Plinlimmon.*

*Lady Plin.* I beg you will put on your beft looks and fit patiently to the painter, that Lord Melcourt may have a good refemblance of you.

*Mifs Plin.* What does he want my picture for? will he not fee me morning, noon, and night? 'tis not likely he fhould forget my face: or is it to hang me in effigy, in cafe I fhould run away from him?

*Lady Plin.* It is ufual for the bride to prefent her portrait to the bridegroom, fo I beg you will make no difficulty about it.

*Enter Lord* MELCOURT *and* Mr. FANCY.

*Mr. Fancy.* I hope I do not intrude upon your Ladyfhip?

*Lady Plin.* By no means.

*Mr. Fancy.* This is the hour your Ladyfhip appointed, and I confefs I am impatient to commence the flattering tafk, but to do juftice to the charms of that young lady, no pencil can have the prefumption.

*Mifs Plin.* The painter, I find, mamma, fays finer things than the lover.

*Lord Mel.* It is part of his profeffion to talk the language of bombaft, and inordinate adulation: It becomes my fituation to fhew refpect, a delicate referve, a genuine but not an importunate attachment, a calm not a tempeftuous folicitude; in one word, a filent adoration.

*Mifs Plin.* Silent enough! egad I believe your adoration has a lock jaw.

*Lady Plin.* Fie child! don't talk fo ridiculoufly; pray Mr. Fancy in what coftume fhall my daughter be drawn?

*Mr. Fancy.* Perhaps Mifs Plinlimmon will point out herfelf what character fhe prefers.

*Mifs Plin.* I hope Mr. Fancy will give my

face

face a good character, for it has done no harm.

*Mr. Fancy.* I afk your pardon, it has done a great deal of harm ; but if my opinion was confulted, I fhould recommend to Mifs Plinlimmon to be painted in the attitude of reading.

*Mifs Plin.* I fhould like to be drawn reading, for I know I have a pretty down-caft look

*Lady Plin.* I muft not forget to inform you that all the females of the Plinlimmon's have had a family mole, a little above the left eye, for thefe two centuries : Now Ifabella's is too complicated with the eye-brow ; perchance you can make fome flight alteration.

*Mr Fancy.* By the omnipotence of the pencil we can raife the beauty fpot, and place it in view.

*Lord Mel.* But is not that departing from reality ? is it not a deceit ? a kind of pencil lie ?

*Mr. Fancy.* It is only changing the local refemblance, it is at the worft a fkilful and elegant inaccuracy ; the beauty-fpot is there, I make no addition to what nature has already done, I only bring to the eye of admiration, what her Ladyfhip informs me nature has rather removed from the fight.

*Lady Plin.* I declare Mr. Fancy, you defend yourfelf moft ingenioufly, does he not my Lord ?

*Lord Mel.* Moft fkilfully indeed !

*Mr. Fancy.* I have taken a much greater licence than this, without feeling any reproach of confcience ; for example, when I had the honor of drawing Lady Frizlerump, I broke the immeafurable length of her bald buff forehead, by introducing two moles and a patch, the patch you know is a thing ad libitum, and as I knew Lady Frizlerump had a mole on each fhoulder, I removed them from their native fpot, (they were well worth the carriage) and I placed them in a more confpicuous fituation ; there is no great deceit in this, it is only
a kind

a kind of tranfplanting, which ought to be as allowable in painting as in gardening.

*Lord Mel.* Well ladies, you perceive how fportfully Mr. Fancy difcourfes, he has a mind to give you a fpecimen of his manner of entertaining his company, when they are fitting to him.

*Lady Plin.* But I think, before we come to any determination about the drefs, it would be proper to confult the attic tafte of Lady Bellair.

*Mr. Fancy.* Moft affuredly, you may fhew her thefe miniatures which I have lately finifhed. This is the portrait of Mifs Harelip, *(gives the miniatures)* which attracted the public eye the laft exhibition. This is only a profile of Mifs Woolfack, the Judge's daughter.

*Lady Plin.* I will not detain you any longer at prefent.

*M. Fancy.* I will wait upon your Ladyfhip, whenever you will favour me with your commands.
(*Exit* Mr. Fancy.

*Mifs Plin.* But why does your Lordfhip wifh fo much to have my picture, fince I am to live with you? do you want me duplicated? don't you think one Mifs Plinlimmon will be enough for you?

*Lord Melcourt.* The mutual exchange of pictures, is one of the etiquettes of modern marriages.

*Lady Plin.* Marriage itfelf may be faid to be a mutual exchange of attention, Indulgence, and affection.

*Mifs Plin.* In this mutual exchange, pray my Lord, inform me which of us two will be the gainer?

*Lord Mel.* If there is any calculation to be made, I am undoubtedly the gainer.

*Mifs Plin.* give me leave to calculate my loffes; in marrying your Lordfhip I lofe my name---I lofe the fociety of papa and mamma---I fhall perhaps, lofe my fhape---and perhaps, in time, lofe my reputation.

*Lady*

*Lady Plin.* Peace to that flippant tongue of
yours, you are trying his Lordfhip's patience before the time.   A I muft carry thefe miniatures to
Lady Bellair, your Lordfhip will excufe my leaving you---Ifabella go to your papa---

(*Exeunt Lady* PLINLIMMON *and
Mifs* PLINLIMMON.

*Lord Mel.* Heaven and earth! What a family
am I going to be connected with! But I muft not
paufe upon that thought, it would almoft lead me
to diftraction.

(*Exit Lord* MELCOURT.

SCENE---*Lady* BELLAIR'S *Apartment.*

*Lady* BELLAIR---*Lady* PLINLIMMON.

*Lady Bell.* Here is a miniature of myfelf, which
was drawn when I was married, I think the drefs
would fuit Mifs Plinlimmon.

*Lady Plin.* (*Taking the miniature.*) 'Tis beautiful, nor could it be otherwife, while it prefumed
to have any refemblance of your Ladyfhip---but
you juft now mentioned your marriage, I know
that you and Lord Bellair were feparated not
long after; interefted as I am in whatever relates to your Ladyfhip, do not imagine it is mere
curiofity that folicits fome illuftration upon that
point.

*Lady Bell.* I am ready to give you every information, and the more fo, as ill-nature, that monotonous and dull commentator, may have conftrued
our feparation in her invariable manner.

*Lady Plin.* I am all attention.

*Lady Bell.* Lord Bellair, fomewhat advanced in
years, palled, and fatiated with the pleafures of the
town, began to meditate a retreat; but before he
retired into the country, from which he was never

E                                to

to return, he ranged through all the gay fcenes of public refort, to find a youthful affociate, to accompany him in his retirement.

*Lady Plin.* Your myfterious hiftory begins to unfold itfelf; the beauteous flower that flourifhed in the bright funfhine of admiration, grew pale and cheerlefs when it was tranfplanted to the folitary gloom of the country.

*Lady B.* I muft confefs your Ladyfhip's extemporary apologue comprifes my little ftory, and makes my continuation unneceffary.

*Lady Plin.* Not at all---I beg you will continue your interefting narrative.

*Lady B.* Lord Bellair, amidft the innumerable beauties, that at once attracted and bewildered his choice, threw at length his felecting glance upon me.

*Lady Plin.* His choice did honor to his tafte.

*Lady B.* It did not however contribute to his happinefs---the fingle voice of my reluctance was loft in the chorus of approbation that refounded from all my relations and friends---I then fummoned all the fortitude I was capable of, and took a courageous leave of the town---adieu, I cried, to the flattery of men---to the pleafing envy of the women---adieu to balls---adieu to the delight of charioteering in a phaeton through St. James's Street every morning---adieu to the eafy inftructions of the town, to the contemplation of manners in caracature-fhops, to the reading of Shakefpear upon canvafs, and to the ftudy of the Englifh hiftory upon walls---the fatal hour arrived--- the carriage was at the door---

*Lady Plin.* You really excite my compaffion! What enfued when you reached the ancient family feat?

*Lady B.* Say rather the family vault!---I wrapt myfelf up in my refignation, as in a winding fheet, and thought to have buried myfelf in a hufband---
the

the fates decreed otherwife: I broke forth from
the ponderous marble, beneath which I was quiet-
ly inurned, and am come again to refide among
the living.

*Lady Plin.* The world is a confiderable gainer
by enjoying you once more. Fortunate was the
ftorm that blew fuch a flower upon the lap of fociety. But whence arofe that ftorm? Did it arife
from Lord Bellair's ill-temper? however, I am
not curious; indeed I can partly guefs: the foli-
tude of the country, faintly checquered by the vifits of the apothecary, and the vicar's wife; his
Lordfhip's fulfome fondnefs---his odious ap-
proaches---

*Lady B.* My dear Lady Plinlimmon, you are
going on fo rapidly! It is of no ufe to reckon the
flight imperceptible threads of difcontent, which
grew at length into a cable. Behold me reftored
to independence, fufficiently affluent, and almoft
as happy as a widow.

*Lady Plin.* May nothing interrupt the happinefs
you poffefs, and which you deferve! Before I had
the honour of your acquaintance, I heard your
merits highly extolled.

*Lady B.* I am exceedingly obliged to thófe perfons who have fmoothed my path to your Ladyfhip's partiality. But to whom am I indebted?

*Lady Plin.* The perfons I allude to are friends
of your Ladyfhip, and are neighbours of our's in
Wales; they were in town laft winter: I mean
Mrs. Vandal and her fifter.

*Lady B.* Yes! I recollect thofe old tapeftry
figures. But you muft not imagine there was any
intimacy between us! I endured them at my toilet.
They may be reckoned, if you pleafe, among my
morning friends, but you may be fure I never ac-
knowledged the creatures in an evening.

*Lady Plin.* That is charming! I fhall acquire
under

under your aufpices the fafhionable difcriminations.
The morning and evening friend is a happy dif-
tinction.    But I fear I am trefpaffing upon your
time.                              *(Offering to go.*

*Lady B.* I will wait upon you immediately.
With your permiffion, I will fend to the company
to affemble in your book-room, where we will fix
upon the plan of this evening's amufement.

*(Exit Lady* PLINLIMMON.

SCENE.---*Book-Room.*

*Enter Lord* MELCOURT---*Mr.* PHRENSY.

*Lord Mel.* We will wait till Lady Plinlimmon
comes, as fhe wifhes extremely to commence a
literary acquaintance with you.

*Mr. Phrenfy.* She is comely, faith! I do not
diflike her perfon.

*Lord Mel.* She is the Ruben's ftyle.

*Mr. Phrenfy.* I hear her coming.

*Enter Lady* PLINLIMMON.

*Lady Plin.* I hope, gentlemen, you have not
been here long.   I feel myfelf peculiarly diftinguifhed in the defire I underftand you expreffed of
forming an acquaintance with me. A man of your
talents is not to be met with in every houfe.

*(Mr.* PHRENSY *bows very low.*

*Lord Mel.* That bow fays more than a pompous
train of words.

*Lady Plin.* I am not infenfible to its eloquence;
it flatters me as much as a dedication.   Pray, fir,
are you engaged in any work at prefent?

*Mr. Phrenfy.* I am only fuperintending a new
edition

edition of the works of a dear friend, whom I have lately loft---the immoŗtal Claſſical Phrenſy !

*Lord Mel.* While Mr. Tombſtone is expatiating on the merits of his departed friend, I will call upon Sir Pepper, and return in a few minutes.

*Lady Plin.* Pray do! and bring Sir Pepper, and Iſabella along with you; the company is to rendezvous here. (*Exit Lord* MELCOURT.) Indeed, ſir, it is very amiable in you to ſupprefs the effuſions of your own powers, to attend to the intereſt of another.

*Mr. Phrenſy.* It is not ſo much attending to the intereſt of my friend, as it is conſulting the intereſt of the nation, while I am preparing this noble edition of his works for the general delight.

*Lady Plin.* But I have been ſo unfortunate as never to hear of Phrenſy's name.

*Mr. Phrenſy.* What! never heard of Claſſical Phrenſy, Eſq. ?

*Lady Plin.* No! I proteſt I never heard his name till you pronounced it.

*Mr. Phrenſy.* Let me tell you, Lady Plinlimmon, if the rays of his genius have not pierced the denſe atmoſphere of Wales, that invelopes your mountains---

*Lady Plin.* Mr. Tombſtone, you alarm me! I had no idea of degrading your friend. I will promote the ſubſcription among all my acquaintance, and do every thing in my power to atone for my ſeeming diſreſpeƈt.

*Mr. Phrenſy.* I am calm again : but you will excuſe a little warmth in favour of a perſon who is as dear to me as myſelf. We were inſeparable ; we never differed upon the ſmalleſt point ; if one ſpoke, the other liſtened ; if one ſlept, the other nodded.

*Lady Plin.* Ah! ſuch a friendſhip is ſeldom to be found. I can aſſure you, ſir, the warmth that
                                                            juſt

juſt now broke from you has only ſerved to exalt me in your eſteem; and, as a proof of what I am ſaying, I beg I may lay the corner-ſtone of our acquaintance with this little brilliant.

*(Gives him a ring.*

*Mr. Phrenſy.* This generoſity ſubdues me.

*Lady Plin.* Let the ring be as a paſſport to this apartment at all times. And when you are at leiſure, I ſhould wiſh to take ſome leſſons of bo-tany under your direction. Lord Melcourt in-forms me, that every ſcience is within the range of your mind.

*Mr. Phrenſy.* I ſhall be happy in obeying your commands.

*Lady Plin.* You think, ſir, that botany is a pro-per occupation for a female mind?

*Mr. Phrenſy.* Nothing ſo proper. Give me leave to cite a couplet, compoſed by my lamented friend, applicable to this ſubject. It is a happy couplet; he ſent it to Lady Nightſhade, who is well verſed in the loves of the plants; it runs thus:

> Delightful emblem of her ſofter power,
> A woman's proper ſtudy is a flower.

*Lady Plin.* Exquiſite couplet! What a great man your friend was!

*Mr. Phrenſy.* The confidence you place in me; this little twinkling monitor of your kindneſs; your affability; every thing prompts, inclines, urges, commands, compels me to undeceive you.

*Lady Plin.* To undeceive me? What can you mean, Mr. Tombſtone?

*Mr. Phrenſy.* I am not Mr. Tombſtone; it is an aſſumed name; a veil to cover me for certain purpoſes.

*Lady Plin.* What purpoſes? Who are you?

*Mr. Phrenſy.* Burſting from my concealment,

like Æneas from his cloud, know that I am Claſſical Phrenſy! 'Tis Phrenſy ſpeaks! 'tis Phrenſy
kneels! 'tis Phrenſy's lips now touch this hand!

*Lady Plin.* I did really imagine you was ſome
great perſonage in diſguiſe. But explain the myſ-
tery of all this.

*Mr. Phrenſy.* Envy, and her train have of late
carried on ſo atrocious a war againſt me, that I have
been perſuaded to ſham a retreat, and give out that
I am dead.

*Lady Plin.* Excellent idea!

*Mr. Phrenſy.* In the mean time, I am collecting
ſubſcriptions, and ſhall return triumphantly to life,
under the cover of a ſuperb edition of all my
works.

*Lady Plin.* I comprehend you perfectly, and am
delighted with the confidence you repoſe in me.

*Mr. Phrenſy.* The family, Mr. Faſhion, the
painter, who is my particular friend, are the only
perſons in the world who are intruſted with this literary ſecret.

*Lady Plin.* I ſhall be as ſilent as Helicon.

*Mr. Phrenſy.* The Heliconian ſtream is apt to
babble; it would be more accurate to ſay, as ſilent
as Lethe.


*Enter Sir* PEPPER, *Miſs* PLINLIMMON, *Lord* MEL-
COURT, *and Mr.* FASHION.


*Lady Plin.* This is the gentleman, Sir Pepper,
whom Lord Melcourt ſpeaks ſo highly of.

*Sir P. Plin.* I am Mr. Tombſtone's moſt obedient. My wife is fond of literature; you will
find her verſed in ſome of the beſt authors. She
is fond of converſing with the dead; or, to ſpeak
more properly, with the living dead.

*Mr.*

*Mr. Phrenfy.* Her Ladyſhip was converſing with the living dead when you entered.

*Lady Plin.* And I muſt add, a favourite author.

*Sir P. Plin.* Is your Lordſhip determined to ſet out for Ireland as ſoon as the ceremony is over ?

*Lord Mel.* The reaſon that compels me to leave you ſo ſoon is the buſineſs I have there, which demands immediate diſpatch.

*Sir P. Plin.* I am ſurpriſed Mr. Conſcience, the lawyer, is not yet come with the writings.

*Lord Mel.* He will certainly be here today.

*Miſs Plin.* What matters, whether or no the lawyer comes ? I wiſh poor Taffey, we left on the road was arrived, for it is the parſon who ſpeaks the prologue to Love's play.

*Mr. Faſh.* Aptly obſerved! but the nuptial play, Miſs Plinlimmon, is ſometimes a tragi-comedy! the dialogue frequently uncouth, vehement, and boiſterous,  What do you think your's will be ?

*Miſs Plin.* Oh! our's will be a gay farce of three acts.


*Enter Lady* BELLAIR.


*Lady B.* Now we are all aſſembled, let the maſter of the ceremonies inſtruct us what we are to do.

*Lord Mel.* The carriages are at the door ; ſuppoſe we take an airing through the park, and lounge at the different buildings.

*Lady B.* Let me be miſtreſs of the revels for this evening. We will imagine the phaetons are triumphal cars, and they ſhall convey us to the temple of Mars, where Mr. Tombſtone ſhall read to the company his new tranſlation of the Battle of the Frogs.

*Lady*

*Lady Plin.* Excellent! I love analogy.

*Lady B.* And as your Ladyſhip is fond of analogy, we will take ſome whipt ſyllabub in the pavi-
lion of friendſhip, and regale ourſelves with ice-
creams in the temple of Hymen.

*Mr. Faſh.* A little ſevere, I think.

*Lord Mel.* "Where more is meant then meets
the ear." *(Offering bis band to Miſs* PLINLIMMON.
*(Exeunt.*

END OF THE SECOND ACT.

A C T

# ÀCT III.

SCENE---*The Temple of Hymen. The Company eating Ice-Creams.*

*Sir* PEPPER PLINLIMMON, *Miſs* PLINLIMMON, *Lord* MELCOURT, *Mr.* FASHION *and Lady* BELLAIR.

*Sir P. Plin.* I think, my Lord, this Temple of Hymen, the moſt beautiful building in your park?

*Mr. Faſh.* This ice is excellent!

*Miſs Plin.* Cold food for the Temple of Hymen---

*Mr. Faſh.* 'Tis not the only food!

*Miſs. Plin.* You mean bread and cheeſe, and kiſſes.

*Lord Mel.* I beg, Lady Bellair, you will check your cicifbeo, Mr. Faſhion, and not let him libertiniſe with my Diana.

*Lady B.* What pretence can I have to reſtrain him? Faſhion is like the air; a chartered libertine, free to play with every flower.

*Miſs Plin.* Egad he ſhan't play with me tho'!

*Lady B.* Tell me, my dear, why did your mamma leave us ſo abruptly?

*Miſs*

*Miſs Plin.* Mamma, I fancy has had enough of the Temple of Hymen.

*Sir P. Plin.* Your Ladyſhip perceives this ſpoiled child, has the liberty of ſaying what ſhe pleaſes. My wife is gone with her ingenious friend, to ſtudy botany.

*Lady B.* I ſhould be ſorry to conſtrain her Ladyſhip.

*Sir P Plin.* Be ſo good as to inform me, who fancied theſe decorations? Are they indebted to the hand of any foreign artiſt?

*Lord Mel.* There is no occaſion to apply to foreign auxiliaries, for the purpoſes of elegant art---the native growth of our ſoil, amply ſupplies the demands of taſte in every department.

*Sir P. Plin.* This relievo, is happily executed! come here, Iſabella, you underſtand mythology. Here is hymen, attended by a group of cupids? Do you conceive the allegoric meaning of the artiſt?

*Miſs Plin.* Perfectly! Here is Hymen, with a torch in his hand, that is, I ſuppoſe to light the bride and bridegroom home. And the dear little cupids I ſuppoſe, foretell the children.

*Sir P. Plin.* Ridiculous! You pervert every thing by your diſtorted applications! But explain the remainder---you ſee night perſonated following Hymen, ſhe throws o'er her frame a mantle ſtudded with ſtars, and among the ſtars, appears a creſcent---

*Miſs Plin.* The mantle ſtudded with ſtars, deſignates the holy ſtillneſs and unruffled union of the marriage ſtate.

*Sir P. Plin.* Very well indeed.

*Miſs Plin.* And the creſcent denotes the honey-moon--

*Sir P. Plin.* There you relapſe into your abſurdity---

Mr.

*Mr. Faſh.* Miſs Plinlimmon will perhaps do me the honor to explain this compartment---here is Hymen, binding a ſhepherd and a ſhepherdeſs with a chain of flowers.

*Miſs Plin.* It is your turn now, you ſhall explain this---

*Mr. Faſh.* Upon my word, I think this a moſt excellent allegory, and illuſtrates well the ſhort triumph of matrimony---the chain of roſes is eaſily broken, and the roſes ſoon fade.

*Lord Mel.* Faſhion ſpeaks the language of an inveterate batchelor, yet every thing in nature condemns his ſarcaſm : the birds, that make this grove re-echo with their harmony, what are all their ſongs, but ſo many hymns in honor of the married ſtate.

*Mr. Faſh.* I aſk your pardon, Lord Melcourt. The economy of your grove, will not aſſiſt your argument, in defence of Hymen, for every feathered couple who were ſo happy the laſt ſpring are now divorced, and all the harmony and love, which now reign in your woods is the reſult of ſeparation and of new engagements.

*Lord Mel.* Truce to your licentious inſinuations, to purify the temple that has been ſo profaned, I entreat Miſs Plinlimmon to favor us with the ſong in honor of Hymen, with which ſhe enchanted the company laſt night---

*Miſs Plin.* I am ready to comply with your requeſt.

*Sir P. Plin.* With your Ladyſhip's permiſſion, I will go and look for the botaniſts.

*Lady B.* He is poſitively jealous (*aſide.*)---Indeed Sir Pepper, you muſt not go, till you have heard the ſong.

*Sir P. Plin.* I am all obedience.

*The SONG, by Miss* PLINLIMMON.

## I.

Oh young affection's glowing train
By mutual fond endearment won!
At Hymen's altar claim the chain
That twines two willing hearts in one!

## II.

Have ye not seen in Flora's bower,
Two roses on one stem respire?
So form'd by passion's blending power,
Two hearts are thron'd on one desire.

*Sir P. Plin.* I presume, I have now your Lady-ship's leave to wait upon the botanists.

*Mr. Fash.* Sir Pepper, you will only interrupt the scholar, in the study of nature---the eminent professor, under whom Lady Plinlimmon is now acquiring a new science, would wish not to be deranged.

*Sir P. Plin.* Very likely---nevertheless, I shall make them a visit.

*Lady B.* We will accompany you to the house.
                                    *(Exeunt omnes*

SCENE

SCENE---*Book-Room.*

*Lady* PLINLIMMON *and Mr.* PHRENSY, *at a table covered with plants and flowers.*

*Lady Plin.* What a wonderful fyftem have you brought me acquainted with? I never could have conceived there were fuch aftonifhing things in nature, as male and female flowers---

*Mr. Phrenfy.* I have moft affuredly, let your Ladyfhip a little into Flora's fecrets.

*Lady Plin.* Male and female flowers! I am petrified! But tell me, learned profeffor, when the flowers are at a diftance from one another, how they communicate their mutual paffion?

*Mr. Phrenfy.* There nature interpofes her happieft ftratagem! She calls her weftern gales, her amorous zephyrs, and they on their fragrant wings convey the lovers to each other.

*Lady Plin.* Now, Sir, as you have led me, as it were, behind the curtain into Flora's green-room, I confefs, I am not much edified at the morals of the plants? Indeed the flowers appear to be an abandoned profligate race---here is a honey fuckle, which you fay contains five males, and only one female---this modeft fnow-drop, you tell me, has fix hufbands---

*Mr. Phrenfy.* Indeed, nature has been rather partial to your fex in her economy of plants.

*Lady Plin.* Poor things! What a pity it is they are not endowed with fenfibility!

*Mr. Phrenfy.* I have obferved, fince the ladies of fafhion have applied to the ftudy of botany, they are not only ambitious of rivaling the flowers in beauty, but they have alfo endeavoured in fome degree to rival them in their other prerogatives.

*Lady Plin.* Take care, Mr. Phrenfy; you are
growing

growing cenforious. (*Enter Sir* PEPPER PLIN-LIMMON.) You cannot imagine, Sir Pepper, how delighted I am with the beautiful and fublime fcience of botany!

*Sir P. Plin.* Indeed!

*Lady Plin.* This learned gentleman has raifed, as it were, the veil of nature, and has revealed to me fome of her fecrets; and I muft own, fecrets that excite my aftonifhment. According to the illuf-trations of this learned profeffor, the chalice of every flower is a kind of a houfe of bad fame.

*Sir P. Plin.* (*ircnically*) Then a lady of your unfpotted virtue ought to fhrink, as the fenfitive-plant, from a ftudy that prefents to you nothing but fcenes of immorality.

*Lady Plin.* There can be no harm in gratifying a literary curiofity. But I affure you, Sir Pepper, I fhall be apt to think it is not extremely decent to wear a nofegay!

*Sir P. Plin.* If you would read the delightful poem of the Loves of the Plants, you need not give this gentleman any further trouble. At pre-fent I muft take the liberty of defiring him to leave us alone, as I have fomething to communicate to you in private.

*Mr. Phrenfy.* I obey your commands. In our next lecture we will expatiate on the dews that re-frefh the flowers at night.

(*Exit Mr.* PHRENSY.

*Lady Plin.* Well, Sir Pepper, what have you to communicate? Nothing I prefume very entertain-ing?

*Sir P. Plin.* You now receive a pofitive order, not to admit that literary fop any more into your ftudy:

*Lady Plin.* What, Sir Pepper! When the ray of knowlege begins to dawn, muft it expire at your uncreating word?

*Sir P. Plin.* Your Ladyfhip's metaphorical ex-preffions

preſſións have no effect upon me, and give me leave to obſerve, that I have always found you refractory and uncomplying with any requeſts.

*Lady Plin.* How can you be ſo unjuſt? Where is the wife throughout Wales that is more complacent? Did I ever refuſe to comply with a requeſt of yours, from January to January? Indeed, Sir Pepper, I might complain of the very few indulgences you ever granted me---

*Sir P. Plin.* Dare you complain of my want of indulgence, when there is not a whim, that I have not always been ready to indulge you in! When the gardening parſon from England came to us laſt year, did I not ſubmit to have the front of my old foreſt, cicatriſed into clumbs like large pies? Did he not fling a confining belt, as he called it, round my place! As if he thought the hills, vales and woods were going to run away! Did I not let him, to pleaſe you, zig zag the avenue in ſuch a manner, that I could hardly find the way to my own houſe?

*Lady Plin.* You muſt allow that Plinlimmon Caſtle, wanted a touch of the modern bard.

*Sir P. Plin.* Then I was obliged to endure his perpetual panegyric upon himſelf! How he was admitted to all the great tables in town? How he choſe a picture for this Lord---and a fan for that Lady---

*Lady Plin.* However, his viſit was not long, he ſtayed with us but a little month.

*Sir P. Plin.* If it had not been for the death of the french cook, he would have been at Plinlimmon Caſtle at this moment.

*Lady Plin.* Do you chooſe to put my patience to any further trial?

*Sir P. Plin.* Recall, if you pleaſe, the phyſician from the north, who came a practiſe-hunting into wales, did he not come twice a day to the
castle

Caſtle to brace your nerves; was not this another indulgence? There you paſſed day after day, lan- guiſhing on a ſopha! Then the room for ſooth was darkened. As you could endure only a kind of twilight, which you called *a jour doux*; then I was never to be admitted, becauſe I ſpoke ſo loud.

*Lady B.* The doctor ſaid you was too boiſter- ous, Sir Pepper, for the chamber of a valetudina- rian, notwithſtanding your incredulity concerning the bad ſtate of my nerves, at that time, I can aſſure you, that it was to the ſopha, and to the doctor, that I owe---

*Sir P. Plin.* More than you will chooſe to allow.

*Lady Plin.* Don't be ſcurrilous, Sir Pepper.

*Sir P. Plin.* Then there was the fencible colo- nel, but I have done. Let me only entreat you not to complain any more of my not granting you any indulgences! Zounds, madam, the Pope at Rome could not have granted you more indul- gences than I have. But no more, I have only to beg of you to ſtay here till I return with ſome papers for you to ſign, and which Lord Melcourt and Mr. Faſhion are to witneſs.

(*Exit Sir* PEPPER PLINLIMMON.

*Lady Plin.* Never was a perſon of delicate feel- ings ſo thrown away as I was when I conſented to be the wife of Sir Pepper.

*Enter Mr.* PHRENSY.

*Mr. Phrenſy.* I watched Sir Pepper out, I heard him go along the gallery muttering, as if he was much diſpleaſed, I am afraid he has been endeavouring to ruffle your angelic temper.

*Lady Plin.* He has abſolutely impoſed his com- mands upon me not to receive your viſits.

*Mr. Phrenſy.* I rejoice to hear it.

*Lady Plin.* What do you mean Mr. Phrenſy?

Mr.

*Mr. Phrenfy.* Prohibition, like a glafs of bitters, ftimulates the appetite and awakens our partialities: I dare fay, I now appear more amiable to your Ladyfhip than I did before.

*Lady Plin.* I confefs, at leaft, your prefumption does not offend me; but I am forry to inform you that you muft not ftay with me at prefent; Sir Pepper is returning immediately, and Lord Melcourt and Mr. Fafhion are coming with him.

*Mr. Phrenfy.* They cannot be here fo foon--- Mr Fafhion was juft now in earneft converfation with Lady Bellair in the long cathedral arbor, and Lord Melcourt was---

*Lady Plin.* You are miftaken---for I hear them coming! What can be done! It is too late to efcape---you muft not take refuge in the bed-chamber, my blabbing maid is there---conceal yourfelf behind this curtain.

(*Lets down the curtain that hangs*
*over the bookfhelves.*

*Mr. Phrenfy.* (*Peeping from behind the curtain.*) I cannot at leaft want entertainment where there are fo many books.

*Lady Plin.* How can you be jocular now? You fee the agitation I am in---


*Enter Sir* PEPPER PLINLIMMON, *Lord* MELCOURT
*and Mr.* FASHION.


*Sir P. Plin.* Thefe gentlemen will have the goodnefs to be witneffes to your figning this paper.

*Lord Mel.* How does your Ladyfhip proceed in the ftudy of botany.

*Lady Plin.* At the defire of Sir Pepper, I have laid afide the thoughts of botany, for the prefent.

*Lord Mel.* It is a pity your Ladyſhip ſhould not avail yourſelf of the advantage of being under the ſame roof with ſo eminent a profeſſor.

*Mr. Faſh.* A perſon of your Ladyſhip's abilities would have made a rapid progreſs under ſo ſkilful a director: he has a way of bringing his ſcholars forward in a very ſhort time.

*Sir P. Plin.* He has the way of bringing himſelf forward in a very ſhort time. Be ſo good as to ſign your name. (*Offering the paper.*) You keep theſe Gentlemen waiting.

*Mr. Faſh.* I am ſure we have nothing better to do than converſe with this learned Lady.

*Lady Plin.* You are very obliging; but I will not any longer intrude on your time.

(*She writes her name---Then Lord* MEL-
COURT *and Mr.* FASHION *ſign.*

*Mr. Faſh.* Pray, Lord Melcourt, have you a Virgil on thoſe ſhelves behind the curtain? Tombſtone and I had a diſpute about a paſſage in the fourth book.

*Lord Mel.* No! That is a mere lady's library, nothing but moderns---I ran up a few ſhelves, and furniſhed them with ſome every-day volumes for the convenience of any lady who might occupy theſe apartments.

*Lady Plin.* Mr. Faſnion, there may be a Virgil behind the curtain; but not the Virgil you mean.

*Mr. Faſh.* You allude to the tranſlation; no, that will not do; I want to conſult the original.

*Lady Plin.* Then you muſt have recourſe to the library below.

*Lord Mel.* But why does your Ladyſhip drop that curtain over the books?

*Lady Plin.* I found it hanging, and I make it a rule to leave things exactly as I find them.

*Sir P. Plin.* The curtain, my dear, I think was up juſt now, when I was with you.

*Lady*

*Lady Plin.* Was it, my dear? I do not recollect.---very true, it was: The fun played fo powerfully upon the books, I was afraid it would tarnifh the beautiful bindings, fo I dropt the curtain---

*Mr. Fafh.* I love beautiful bindings, and typographical luxury. Pray let me be favoured with the fight of the books.

*Lady Plin.* Not worth your infpection---a mere female library, and authors for women.

*Lord Mel.* Allow me to indulge Fafhion's curiofity. As for the fun's fpoiling the books, it matters not, when the bindings are the worfe for wear, the books may have new bindings; a well-bound book is not like a lady's reputation, which once foiled, can never--- *(Draws up the curtain---difcovers Mr. PHRENSY)* There was, indeed, a Virgil behind the curtain!

*Mr. Fafh.* An author for a lady!

*Lord Mel.* But not fo well bound as Fafhion expected.

*Mr. Phrenfy.* Gentlemen, you may laugh if you pleafe, but we enterprifing fellows are now and then expofed to thefe untoward difcoveries. They are inevitable incidents in the comedy of life. This is an incident---

*Sir P. Plin.* Arrogant pedant! If this was not Lord Melcourt's houfe, my cane would chaftife your infolence.

*Lady Plin.* I affure my dear, this gentleman had received my commands not to enter thefe apartments any more; at that inftant I heard you returning.

*Mr. Phrenfy.* And to fave you from an object fo difagreeable as myfelf, I fecreted myfelf behind that curtain.

*Sir P. Plin.* Daring wretch! what is it you mean? Do you prefume to make the perfonal attractions

tractions of that lady the object of your bold pre-
tenfions ?

*Lady Plin.* Well, Sir Pepper, fince we are
among friends, I give you my word, that if ever I
could be perfuaded to deviate from the path of de-
corum, and make a little *faux pas,* it fhould not
be with a literary perfon.

*Mr. Fafh.* Your Ladyfhip is perfectly right.
The literary heroes are not renowned in the an-
nals of gallantry ; a bookworm is a poor harmlefs
creature, without a fting,

*Sir P. Plin.* What you fay, Mr. Fafhion, is fenfible and judicious. I have heard it obferved, that
a lieutenant of the guards is more formidable to a
married man, than the whole body of the anti-
quarian fociety. Mr. Tombftone will excufe the
warmth I was juft now furprifed into.

*Mr. Phrenfy.* Pray do not mention it. Your
prohibition with regard to my coming to this apartment fhall be ftrictly obeyed, and I fhall for the
future look for the honour of your Ladyfhip's fociety only in the drawing-room, which you know
is a neutral apartment, and acceffible to every part
of the family.

*Sir P. Plin.* Gentlemen, your obedient. I muft
return with thefe papers. ( *Exit.*

*Lord Mel.* Well, this fcene has ended much better than I expected. The ftorm would have fallen
heavy upon Tombftone, had it not been for your
Ladyfhip's happy farcafm upon the gallantry of the
learned.

*Mr. Phrenfy.* Your Lordfhip need not call me
Tombftone ; her Ladyfhip knows my ftory ; there
is nothing refpecting myfelf that is a fecret to her
Ladyfhip.

*Lord Mel.* I am glad to hear it. But I muft
beg leave to abfent myfelf; I hope your Ladyfhip
will excufe me.

*Lady*

*Lady Plin.* But why will your Lordſhip deprive us of your company?

*Lord Mel.* Conſider, Madam, I am at the eve of being married---my mind is ſo full---I have ſo many things to think of.

*Mr. Phrenſy.* What can your Lordſhip have to think of? every thing flows ſo ſmoothly to your wiſhes---you have no more occaſion to think than a tranſlator.

*Mr. Faſh.* No more he has: and I could undertake to prove that his Lordſhip is a kind of a tranſlator himſelf, and even a tranſlator into various languages.

*Lord Mel.* How do you make that out?

*Mr. Faſh.* I have ſeen you ſometimes in liquor, and then you tranſlate yourſelf into a beaſt.

*Mr. Phrenſy.* Very good!

*Mr. Faſh.* You will ſoon be married, and then you will tranſlate yourſelf into another kind of animal.

*Mr. Phrenſy.* You miſtake, that will not be his own doing.

*Mr. Faſh.* Very true! ſome intimate friend will do that tranſlation for him.

*Lord Mel.* Will not your Ladyſhip take my part againſt theſe profane batchelors?

*Lady Plin.* The arrows theſe gentlemen ſhoot are not dipt in gall.

*Lord Mel.* Nor are their points very keen. But I muſt be going.

*Lady Plin.* As the party is breaking up, ſuppoſe, Mr. Phrenſy, you attend me to the neutral apartment. as you ingeniouſly term it.

*Mr. Phrenſy.* I am at your command.

(*Offers his hand.---Exit with*
Lady PLINLIMMON.

*Lord Mel.* There go two, the moſt ridiculous perſonages!

*Mr. Faſh.* And the beſt ſuited to one another.

*Lord*

*Lord Mel.* I wifh my future bride and I were half as well adapted to one another.

*Mr. Fafh.* What! Melcourt, do you feel faint-hearted?

*Lord Mel.* Faith! I do. The whimficality of the different perfons under this roof, has occafion-ed fome laughing, which has ferved to divert my attention from the main objeƈt. But when my thoughts'reft upon my approaching nuptials, my mind fhrinks from its purpofe.

*Mr. Fafh.* Oh! this is nothing but a vapour fit, a qualm before matrimony; it will pafs away.

*Lord Mel.* Never, never.

*Mr. Fafh.* She is handfome---very rich.

*Lord Mel.* Did fhe poffefs all the barbaric gold of the city, it would not atone for her deficiencies in other refpeƈts.

*Mr. Fafh.* What do you call deficiencies? The little rufticities of her homebred education will difappear in time; fhe will catch the tone of the ftage fhe is entering upon; the continual aƈtion of furrounding example in higher life will wear away her peculiarities, and fhe will infenfibly glide into the general mafs.

*Lord Mel.* You are calm and philofophic; but I cannot be cooled and philofophifed into the ap-proval of what I am fenfible is not ftriƈtly honour-able; which is leading, and as it were betraying a young woman to the altar, for whom I entertain no paffion, no preference, no efteem.

*Mr. Fafh.* Your good nature will prompt you to treat her with civility; her fimplicity will ex-plain your politenefs into love; and the torrent of amufements in town will prevent her prying into your private pleafure-ground.

*Lord Mel.* Fafhion, you talk it well; but I do proteft, if I could be prevailed upon to marry this young woman, difliking her as I do, I fhould feel

an

an internal degradation, that would poifon all my days.

*Mr. Fafh.* What can be done ? it is too late to recede ; the Welch Family will be in an uproar.

*'Lord Mel.* I have a fcheme---a lucky thought occurred this morning. I think I have hit upon a method of efcaping from the chains I have been forging for myfelf ; and in preparing the girl for the event, I fhall contrive to foften her difappointment by a kind of innocent impofition, which will make her believe that the breaking off the intended marriage is her own act.

*Mr. Fafh.* This is at once generous and humane ; to ward off the point that would wound her pardonable vanity in the expectation of being Lady Melcourt. But what is your plan ?

*Lord Mel.* That I will communicate to you in a more private place ; and if my ftratagem fhould not fucceed, I muft then have recourfe to your fuperior invention.  *(Exeunt.*

END OF THE THIRD ACT

A C T

# ACT IV.

*Miss Plin.* (*Reading aloud*)---" Oh! happy state, when souls each other draw". (*Enter Lord* MEL-court.) Your calling upon me, when I am alone, is very kind; I am now convinced, your Lord-ship has a great regard for me.

*Lord Mel.* May I take the liberty of asking, what book has the honor of engaging your atten-tion?

*Miss Plin.* I have been dressing my expectation with love verses. (*Reads*)

" For thee the spouse, prepares the bridal ring,

" For thee white virgins hymeneals sing!"---

But what makes you look so grave, when you are so near being a bridegroom? A little bird sung in my ear, that to-morrow, is to be the happy day, and I suppose your Lordship, is come to inform me of the happy tidings.

*Lord Mel.* No indeed! I did not come for that purpose, I came with another view.

*Miss Plin.* I hope it will not rain to-morrow, there must not be a speck of a cloud, in the skies, on our wedding day.

*Lord Mel* I must beg your serious attention, to

H                              what

what I have to fay to you (*Takes a chair*; *offers her one*; *they fit*)---If I feem a little embarraffed, you will have the goodnefs to excufe me? I think it my duty, to inform you, that when I was laft abroad, I had the misfortune of being introduced to a young Nun who gained my affections, and though that accomplifhed woman is no more---

*Mifs Plin.* If fhe is no more, I have nothing to apprehend, for with all her want of accomplifhments, Ifabella Plinlimmon, muft be fuperior to a dead Nun.

*Lord Mel.* 'Tis not only that---

*Mifs Plin.* Your Lordfhip did not fall in love with the whole convent?

*Lord Mel.* No, no, when I loft my Conftantia, my warm affections, flew to her tomb.

*Mifs Plin.* And when your warm affections have caught cold at her tomb, they will fly back again.

*Lord Mel.* Never, never, with her they have taken up their everlafting refidence.

*Mifs Plin.* Well let them; you and I will make new affections.

*Lord Mel.* (*Afide.*) Nothing will do, fhe is determined to have me.

*Mifs Plin.* What does your Lordfhip fay?

*Lord Mel.* I am afraid, Mifs Plinlimmon, there are other objectionable circumftances relative to myfelf; with all the appearance of affability and condefcenfion, I can affure you, that I am moft vehemently paffionate.

*Mifs Plin.* Matrimony will cure that vice! I have heard my mamma fay, that marriage is a great tamer.

*Lord Mel.* I have alfo the misfortune of walking in my fleep, and I get out of the window, and walk upon the roof of the houfe.

*Mifs Plin.* As long as you do not infift upon my walking with you, I do not call that an objectionable circumftance: and when you are tired of
                                          imhaling

imhaling the night breezes from the top of the houfe, you will find me overjoyed to receive you at your return.

*Lord Mel.* (*Rifing from his chair.*) I fee, Mifs Plinlimmo<sub></sub>, you make a jeft of what my delicate feelings pr mpt me to reveal to you.

*Mifs Plin.* (*Rifing.*) Quite the reverfe; your candour endears you the more to me; and to return you an equivalent of candour and unreferve, on my part, I will unfold to your Lordfhip a fecret, though I am unwilling to difclofe it.

*Lord Mel.* Well, what have you to communicate?

*Mifs Plin.* 'Tis what you would have found out, if I did not reveal it: but in this charming moment of mutual confidence, I cannot refift telling my love, that I have crooked legs;

*Lord Mel.* Crooked legs! The devil.

*Mifs Plin.* Do not let fuch a trifle difcompofe you: my aunt, Lady Waddle, is made juft the fame as I am, and fhe has eleven children.

*Lord Mel.* If you pleafe, Mifs Plinlimmon, we will put an end to this difcourfe.

*Mifs Plin.* If you defire it. We fhall have time enough to talk, when we are man and wife: adieu, I am going to Lady Bellair, and will tell her all that has paffed, in this delightful, confidential intercourfe.

*Lord Mel.* I muft infift upon your not revealing one word, to Lady Bellair, of what I have been faying to you.

*Mifs Plin.* As you pleafe; your Lordfhip will find me through life ftrictly obfervant of your commands.  (*Exit Mifs* PLINLIMMON.

*Lord Mel.* Were my debts and difficulties, treble to what they are, I would not extricate myfelf on the condition of marrying that thing! That vile antithefis! Half a wit, and half an ideot. (*Enter Mr.* FASHION.) Oh! Fafhion, you never came

fo

fo opportunely, I am at a lofs how to act; my fcheme has entirely failed---

*Mr. Fafh.* Then I muft be your pilot to fteer you through this intricate perplexity.

*Lord Mel.* Her ideot fondnefs, increafes with what fhould have excited her difguft.

*Mr. Fafh.* Leave me to conftruct the means of withdrawing from you this girl's partiality, I prefume, I am empowered to fay whatever I pleafe.

*Lord Mel.* You may indulge the utmoft latitude; paint me in whatever colours you choofe;

*Mr. Fafh.* Well, I will endeavour to do my beft for you; I have a good knack, you know, at a caricature.

*Lord Mel.* But do not make me too ridiculous.

*Mr. Fafh.* Remember, you juft now gave me unlimited powers.

*Lord Mel.* Very true; I refign myfelf to your judgment; let me appear abfurd, fickle, prepofterous, any thing, to get rid of this matrimonial engagement.

*Mr. Fafh.* Suppofe while I am unwinding her affections and defires from you, I fhould endeavour to bottom, and twift them round myfelf?

*Lord Mel.* What! you marry her? Are you in earneft? Will you quit your free roving pleafure-boat, for the monotonous hulk of matrimony?

*Mr. Fafh.* Her guineas will decorate and enliven the hulk.

*Lord Mel.* Well, if you can make a profelyte of the girl, you have my full permiffion, and beft wifhes; here is my licenfe, which with a change of a name will ferve your purpofe, and you may get married immediately, without acquainting any of the family of it.

*Mr. Fafh.* I will go, and inform Lady Bellair, of your refolution, and of my project.

*Lord Mel.* I fhould be delighted, if the girl was to take a fancy to you---

*Mr. Fafh.* We fhall fee.                (*Exeunt.*
                                                      SCENE

Scene---*Lady* Bellair's *Apartment.*

*Lady* Bellair---*Miſs* Plinlimmon.

*Lady B.* What you choofe to fay in private, is of no confequence; but before company, I muft infift upon your never mentioning my hufband.

*Miſs Plin.* Then tell me, as we are alone; I long to hear what occafioned the feparation between Lord Bellair and you.

*Lady B.* Reftrain this idle curiofity; it does not become---

*Miſs Plin.* Did your hufband walk in his fleep? Was he in love with a dead nun?

*Lady B.* How wildly you talk!

*Miſs Plin.* Not fo wildly neither; I know what I know; but I will not tell.

*Enter Sir* Pepper Plinlimmon.

*Sir P. Plin.* I take the liberty of calling upon your Ladyfhip to exprefs my uneafinefs that the lawyer from town is not yet arrived, the poft is come in, and I have no information about him.

*Lady B.* Delay is the characteriftic of his order! When that Gray's Inn flug has crawled over, and covered with his black flime an acre of parchment, we fhall fee him here.

*Miſs Plin.* But Mr. Taffey, who is to perform the ceremony, is as neceffary as the lawyer.

*Sir P. Plin.* As for Mr. Taffey, I have a letter from him; he will be here this evening.

*Miſs Plin.* Then all is well! (*Rejoicing extravagantly.---Enter Lord* Melcourt) My Lord! my my Lord! Taffey will be here this evening, and to-morrow I ſhall be the fondeſt of wives!

*Lord Mel.* Flattering as your expeċtancy may be to me, I wiſh you would reſtrain this inordinate exultation.

*Miſs. Plin.* Well, papa, I will go and pack up my fine cloaths, for I ſuppoſe we ſhall ſet out for Ireland immediately after the ceremony. I rejoice to think that Taffey will be here this evening!

                                                         *(Exit.*

*Lord Mel.* *(Aſide to Lady* BELLAIR) Was there ever ſuch a Hottentot?

*Sir P. Plin.* You don't appear, Lord Melcourt, to be ſtruck with the artleſs manner of my girl.

*Lord Mel.* I aſk your pardon, I am exceedingly ſtruck!

*Sir P. Plin.* She has a few ruſticities adhering to her, all which will drop from her, like droſs from gold.

*Lord Mel.* In the crucible of Lady Bellair's refining converſation.

*Sir P. Plin.* Very true. I am certain Lady Bellair would perform miracles on my daughter--- if ſhe pleaſed.

*Lady B.* But why, Sir Pepper, do you doubt my inclination?

*Sir P. Plin.* Becauſe you, fine ladies, diſlike trouble. I will be bold to ſay, that in the courſe of the winter, you never do any thing your inclination, that is to ſay, your vanity does not prompt you to do.

*Lady B.* I aſk your pardon, Sir Pepper.

*Sir P. Plin.* Indulge for once an old man's curioſity, and edify me by recording ſome inſtances where you aċt in oppoſition to the dictates of your inclination.

*Lord Mel.* This is a perfeċt challenge.

*Lady B.* Well, let me recollcċt. I go every other Sunday, in the early part of the evening to

                                                            **an**

an old aunt, who lives at the Antipodes of the fashionable part of the town, and there I retail to her the hiſtoric ſcandal of the fortnight ; and then ſhe reads to me through her green ſpectacles, out of a folio, a ſermon of the laſt century.

*Lord Mel.* I hope, Sir Pepper, you will give Lady Bellair ſome credit for that.

*Lady B.* Then I go once in the winter to the Ancient Muſic.

*Sir P. Plin.* That, I ſuppoſe, is a concert performed by the decayed muſicians.

*Lady B.* Not exactly ſo; it is, however, a very edifying concert, and compoſed of thoſe hoary, venerable notes, that in days of yore delighted the ears of Harry the eighth and Anne Bullen, and is now a very ſuitable recreation for old batchelors, old maids, and emigrant nuns! But to continue the narrative of my mortified inclination: my carriage every morning makes one of the long proceſſion of coaches that beſiege the circulating library in Bond Street.

*Sir P. Plin.* That denotes your Ladyſhip's fondneſs for literature.

*Lady B.* I beg your pardon, Sir Pepper, literature is my averſion; I never look into a book, but I cannot avoid calling every morning at the library; it is a kind of literary tavern, where the waiters are in perpetual demand. A diſh of elegant ſonnets for Miſs Simper; ſatires with a poignant ſauce for Mrs. Grumble; a ſirloin of hiſtory for Lady Sleepleſs; a broil'd devil of private anecdote, highly peppered with ſcandal, for Lady Angelica Worthleſs. It would amuſe you, Sir Pepper, to ſee theſe female academics enter the porch of Hookham College, their cheeks, paled by ſtudy, a little relieved by a thin ſtratum of morning rouge. Then you would wonder at the method the learned profeſſors adopt of ſupplying the impatience of their pupils : for example---one lady
receives

receives the firſt volume of an author, of which ſhe will never enquire for the ſecond; at the ſame time ſhe receives the ſecond volume of another author, of which ſhe has not yet an idea of the firſt.

*Sir P. Plin.* Give me leave to obſerve, this vague method of reading muſt create a kind of chaos, without conſiſtency.

*Lady B.* Conſiſtency is a vulgar word, we do not admit into our vocabulary; and as for the chaos you diſapprove of, I really think there is to be found the whole merit; for this miſcellaneous, variegated, unconnected reading, forms the beautiful dove-tailed, moſaic literature of the female mind.

*Sir P. Plin.* I hope you will allow Lady Plin-limmon to be a brilliant exception to your general deſcription.

*Lady B.* Moſt undoubtedly; I have a long liſt of exceptions. But not to interrupt the narrative of my own memoirs---I am ſometimes obliged to mingle with the elegant mob at a ſale of pictures.

*Sir P. Plin.* A ſale of pictures muſt be very improving. You there frequently meet with the works of the old maſters.

*Lady B.* The ladies of faſhion do not go to auctions for the ſake of the *old* maſters; do they, Lord Melcourt?

*Lord Mel.* No, indeed! A bow from Lord Gauze, a ſmile from Lord Flimſy, or a compliment from Sir Goſſamer Bagatelle, effaces the names of Rembrant, Corregio, and Vandyke!

*Lady B.* However, we play with the catalogue, and we ſtare at the pictures. And I have heard it obſerved, that in the two late celebrated ſales, the love of Vertú made the ladies gaze at ſome pictures, from which their grand-mammas would have turned away.

*Sir P. Plin.* Indeed!

*Lady*

*Lady B.* But then, I will fay for the ladies, that they ftole a glance at thefe pictures, through the medium of their long veils, which you know tranf-mits a kind of drapery, to the paintings! But to proceed, I am under the obligation, fometimes, of getting up in the middle of the night, to be in readinefs, to go to a new play, and with all my precaution, I never can get there before the middle of the fecond act.

*Sir P. Plin.* That is very unlucky.

*Lady B.* Not in the leaft; for I never liften to the play.

*Sir P. Plin.* But does not your talking loud in the firft row, difturb the audience?

*Lady B.* I never occupy the firft row; I place the old ladies, in the firft and fecond row, they have nothing to do, (poor things) but to liften to the play? And then I fit fnug on the laft form, which we call among ourfelves, tattle row, and then perhaps, I am feated between Sir Voluble Prattle, and Colonel Eafy, and we three converfe and titter *a la fourdine,* the whole evening: but I am afraid I grow dull.

*Sir P. Plin.* Quite the reverfe, I affure you; I prefume, your Ladyfhip pays more attention to the opera; the foftnefs of the Italian language, has fomething enchanting to a delicate ear.

*Lady B.* I know nothing of the Italian lan-guage, there is no attaining the knowledge of it, without paffing through the perplexing, jumbling, crofs-roads of a grammar; that would fhake my intellects to pieces.

*Sir P. Plin.* Still the mufic may flatter the ear, though you do not comprehend the words.

*Lady B.* I comprehend the mufic as little as I do the words.

*Sir P. Plin.* It is, then, the dancing I conclude delights you---

*Lady B.* No; the dancing does not particularly interest me; indeed I cannot fee the dancing in my box, for I generally fit with my back to the ftage.

*Sir P. Plin.* As neither the mufic, nor the dancing has any allurement, I fuppofe your Ladyfhip feldom or never goes to the opera.

*Lady B.* I afk your pardon, Sir Pepper, I never omit an opera.

*Sir P. Plin.* What then can be the attraction? I really fee nothing to entice you.

*Lady B.* Is it nothing, Sir Pepper, to lean half out of one's box; with the head inclined to give the eafy feather a more graceful play? which looks a meteor, waving in the air; and which, as the poet fays,

" Allures attention, from the tuneful fcene;

" Gives fops the flutter, and old maids the fpleen."

Is it nothing, Sir Pepper, to have all the opera glaffes levelled at one? To fit in my box, as on a throne, the unrivalled queen of Fopland?

*Lord Mel.* I muft confefs, Lady Bellair, you have an extenfive dominion; Fopland is a very populous country.

*Lady B.* So it is, and what is ftill better, there is not an old man to be found in it.

*Sir P. Plin.* I am forry, I am excluded from being one of your majefty's fubjects?

*Lady B.* Out of regard to your gallantry, I will introduce a bill to naturalife you, Sir Pepper, but not to lofe the thread of my narrative, I muft inform you, that I go once in the winter to an affembly, given by the wife of my phyfician; there all his pale convalefcents ftalk about like ghofts:

*Lord Mel.* And to conclude the defcription; the lemonade is intentionally made fo acid that the doctor is obliged to return all the vifits of his company the next day.

*Sir P. Plin.* Very good indeed.

*Lady B.* You perceive what a mortified life I am obliged to lead.

*Sir P. Plin.* If your historic pencil has drawn a true resemblance, I must confess, a fashionable lady is to me an incomprehensible being. *(Exit.*

*Lady B.* Now we have got rid of the ridiculous baronet, I must assume a graver tone; you know, I can be very serious when occasion demands. The more I see of Sir Pepper's absurd daughter, the more I am sensibly affected at the thought of your approaching nuptials. The long train of peculiar distresses incident to our family, I wish not to see terminated by means so unworthy and ignominous.

*Lord Mel.* I do not comprehend you.

*Lady B.* By marrying a young woman you are ashamed of; our family has been long involved in various difficulties; it has been known to misfortune, but it has never been acquainted with dishonor? Imagine two large portals opening before you, through one of which, you should be obliged to pass! Imagine one presenting to your view a brilliant perspective, a sun streaming from a summer sky, and illuminating an earthly paradise! The other unfolding to your vision, a lowring atmosphere hanging over a blasted heath. Picture to yourself these words, engraved on the first portal; *they who pass through me, must cast away honor.*---Fancy on the other, you behold this inscription---*This road leads, to honorable poverty*; through which of these arches, would you direct your footsteps? Oh! my dear brother, in the agitation you betray, I read your heroic answer.

*Lord Mel.* Before you had communicated your sentiments to me, upon this subject, I had made my reflection, and had resolved, but Mr. Fashion, whom I am glad to see, *(Enter* FASHION.) will

beſt

beſt unfold the plan we had formed together, I refer you to him, the confuſion I am at preſent under, will excuſe my leaving you ſo abruptly.

(*Exit.*

*Mr. Faſh.* Heyday, what is the matter with Melcourt? He ſtalked by me, in dumb ſhew, like a tragedy hero.

*Lady B.* The agitation you perceive he is in, is the honeſt working of nature, it will do him no harm; my brother tells me, you have ſomething to communicate to me.

*Mr. Faſh.* I have, and it is of importance, I was commiſſioned by him, as he did not chooſe to ſpeak himſelf, that he is determined to break off this match.

*Lady B.* He partly intimated his reſolution. But who undertakes to inform the girl of his re-ſolution?

*Mr. Faſh.* That falls to my part in the play.

*Lady B.* What do you propoſe ſaying to the poor girl? How will you open your unpleaſant embaſſy?

*Mr. Faſh.* Not ſo unpleaſant, becauſe I intend to propoſe myſelf.

*Lady B.* Propoſe yourſelf!

*Mr. Faſh.* As I do not occupy ſo high a ſtation in life as Lord Melcourt, I mean, by propoſing myſelf, to be a kind of a parachute, and ſo break, as it were, her fall.

*Lady B.* You are very kind, indeed. You may not perhaps be ſo invincible in the eyes of the young lady as you are in your own.

*Mr. Faſh.* I rely on your friendly aſſiſtance.

*Lady B.* There you are miſtaken. But do not impute my declining to co-operate with you, to a fear that this may be the means of withdrawing your aſſiduities and attentions from me. I hope I act from a more noble impulſe. I am ready to confeſs that the excluſive preference and predilec-

tion

tion you have fhewn me of late, have gratified my
vanity ; but like the waves that beat againſt the
heedleſs rock, they have not fhook my conſtancy
to the man whoſe name I bear.

*Mr. Faſh.* The playful gaiety of your difpoſi-
ţion led me aſtray, and I thought you was delighted
ţo return to ſociety unaccompanied by Lord Bellair.

*Lady B.* I own I have the appearance of airineſs
and levity ; but my gaiety is frequently aſſumed, and
I have recourſe to diſſipation more as a medicine
than a feaſt.

*Mr. Faſh.* As you are ſo kind as to ſpeak to me
in ſo unreſerved a manner, I think it incumbent on
me to declare that I have no inbred averſion to
the girl. I am not ſo faſtidious, ſo difficult, as
Melcourt ; and I will add, that was I to ſucceed,
I would do every thing in my power to contribute
to her happineſs, and give me alſo leave to ſay
that I believe I am not indifferent to her.

*Lady B.* With ſuch honorable ſentiments as
you now aſſure me you entertain, you have my
permiſſion to make the trial. Mutual propenſity,
believe me, is the beſt ſecurity for happineſs. The
ſmiling flowers ſhe ſcatters from her hand can alone
enliven the domeſtic walk ! 'Tis ſhe who diſplays
to the bride and bridegroom that eternal ſpring
which all lovers talk of, but which ſo few expe-
rience ! 'Tis ſhe who gilds and diſſipates the
clouds of care, and pours upon the ſoul the chearful ſunſhine of the mind.             *( Exeunt.*

**END OF THE FOURTH ACT.**

## A C T  V.

*Miſs* PLINLIMMON, *ſitting at a Table, writing.*

I AM glad to find that my letters are finiſhed. I cannot conceive what Mr. Faſhion has to ſay to me in private. Theſe letters will make my friends very happy. (*Enter Mr.* FASHION) You are punctual to your time; I was juſt thinking of you. Mr. Faſhion, you are a perſonable man---I wonder you are not married.

*Mr. Faſh.* The reaſon I am not married, is be-cauſe there is only one Miſs Plinlimmon. But give me leave to tell you, that you are too late for the poſt.

*Miſs Plin.* Theſe letters are not intended for to-day's poſt, nor to morrow's poſt; but they are intended for the poſt the day after the wedding. You muſt know that I am bound by a ſolemn pro-miſe to write two letters the day after my mar-riage, and as we ſhall be on our road to Ireland on that day, and conſequently ſhall have no time to write, I thought it would be a good plan to write beforehand, and date the letters after the wedding, which

which you fee I have done, and have figned myfelf Ifabella Melcourt.

*Mr. Fafh.* Very ingenioufly contrived indeed!
May I take the liberty of afking who this letter
is to?

*Mifs Plin.* It is to Mrs. Evans, an old maiden
aunt, who was always very kind to me. There
are no fecrets, if you pleafe, I will read it to you.

*Mr. Fafh.* I am fure it muft be worth hearing
if it comes from your pen.

*Mifs Plin. (reads)*

" Dear Aunt,
 " Yefterday the holy ceremony was per-
" formed. We all wept---Mamma had an hyf-
" teric---two beautiful tears ftole down the cheek
" of my amiable Lord, and when he put on the
" ring his hand trembled"---

*Mr. Fafh.* But, Mifs Plinlimmon, allow me to
afk, how do you know all this will happen?

*Mifs Plin.* There is always weeping at a wedding, as much as at a funeral.

*Mr. Fafh.* Well, I plead ignorance, for I never
affifted at a wedding.

*Mifs Plin.* Then get your white handkerchief
ready to-morrow morning. But let me fee where
I left off--- *(reads)*

" ---When he put on the ring his hand trem-
" bled. After the ceremony, we fat down to a
" fumptuous collation. We lay at a town whofe
" name I forget. You cannot, dear madam, have
" any conception of his Lordfhip's kindnefs to
" me.

  " I am, dear Aunt,
   " Your thrice happy niece,

    " ISABELLA MELCOURT.

" *Poftcript.* I fhould have written a longer let-
" ter, had I not a bad head-ache."

Mr.

*Mr. Fash.* But permit me to afk, how do you forefee you will have a bad head-ache?

*Mifs Plin.* I heard my mamma-in-law fay that fhe had a terrible head-ache, the day after fhe married, fo 'tis very probable---

*Mr. Fash.* I perceive there is another letter; who is honored with this mark of your remembrance?

*Mifs Plin.* This is to Mifs Bluehofe, member of the female literary fociety at Carnarvon.

*Mr. Fash.* With this lady I fuppofe you affume a higher ftyle.

*Mifs Plin.* I endeavour in this letter to write exactly as Mifs Bluehofe talks---　　(*Reads.*)

" Sweet Academic Friend,

　　" Aurora, yefterday, put on her beft faf-
" fron robe, to affift at our wedding: we are on
" our road to Ireland, my lord, you know, is a na-
" tive of that kingdom, what a delightful country
" muft that be, which produces fuch men? Laft
" night three minutes before twelve, I afcended
" the expecting couch.

*Mr. Fash.* Very happy expreffion that!

*Mifs Plin.* I am glad you are pleafed with it, the expecting couch, is in the manner and ftyle of our academic fociety; but to proceed: (*reads*) " Hiftory informs us, my dear Mifs Bluehofe, of the " bed of Procuftes, of the bed of Ware, of the *Lit* " *de Juftice*, and of the bed of honor; I wonder that " in this learned catalogue, the hiftorian omitted " the bed of Hymen."

*Mr. Fash.* It is an unpardonable omiffion, indeed.

*Mifs. Plin.* Now we have done with the letters, be fo good as to inform me why you look fo ferious? I begin to think, you envy Lord Melcourt---well, if you do, I will tell you, for your comfort, that if I was to be a widow, and had

　　　　　　　　　　　　　　　　　moulted

moulted away my black feathers, that is to fay, when I had fhed my weeds and got rid of my forrow, I really think you would ftand a good chance.

*Mr. Fafh.* You flatter me extremely, but to advert to the fubject, which induced me to beg this private audience, I muft inform you that nothing but the great refpect I entertain for you, could compel me to mention Lord Melcourt, in terms not the moft favourable.

*Mifs Plin.* I know what you allude to, but he has promifed papa, never to touch a card again.

*Mr. Fafh.* I do not allude to his paffion for gaming, I point to quite a different thing.

*Mifs Plin.* I know what you mean there too, he has told me all; he clambers up the roof of the houfe every night.

*Mr. Fafh.* Clambers up the roof of the houfe! I can't tell what he has chofen to communicate to you, but I dare fay, he has not given you any hint of what my regard for you prompts me to reveal; to keep you no longer in fufpenfe, Melcourt does not love you; I can fcarcely fupprefs my indignation, when I behold fo enchanting, fo learned, fo witty a young lady as Mifs Plinlimmon become---

*Mifs Plin.* How kind you are!

*Mr. Fafh.* Become, I fay, the dupe of that indigent peer, who only wifhes to have his debts paid by your fortune. He will look upon you with no greater fenfibility than he does his old banker in the city: he will fet you afide, like an ufelefs piece of lumber.

*Mifs Plin.* You petrify me, Mr. Fafhion! But I have a refource left, which will prevent my being reduced to an ufelefs piece of lumber.

*Mr. Fafh.* And what is that refource?

*Miſs. Plin.* It is a reſource which belongs to the rights of women; a curtain lecture.

*Mr. Faſh.* Oh! that will have no effect.

*Miſs Plin.* I know that my mamma-in-law has frequent recourſe to that expedient.

*Mr. Faſh.* And what has been her ſucceſs? Her nocturnal murmurings, and her loud matin ſong, what have they produced, but an airy, talkative family of bickerings and diſcontent?

*Miſs Plin.* 'Tis very true.

*Mr. Faſh.* I have frequently been aſtoniſhed at Lord Melcourt's cold indifference towards you.

*Miſs Plin.* Indeed he has not ſaid one kind word to me ſince I have been at Melcourt Hall.

*Mr. Faſh.* Then the vehemence of his cha-racter---

*Miſs Plin.* He told me himſelf he was as croſs as the devil.

*Mr. Faſh.* Then I have wondered at the con-tempt with which he preſumes to ſpeak of you.

*Miſs Plin.* I dare ſay he laughs at me behind my back.

*Mr. Faſh.* I have heard him ſay you are an ideot.

*Miſs Plin.* I an ideot! Did he dare call me an ideot? I, who am one of the female academics at Carnarvon! I an ideot, with whom Miſs Bluehoſe correſponds? I an ideot, who have been electri-fied, and magnetiſed! I an ideot, who am ac-quainted with Mr. Omega, the famous Jew bota-niſt, and have feaſted as his houſe upon his He-brew roots?

*Mr. Faſh.* Notwithſtanding all theſe credentials of your wit, you find what he ſays of you.

*Miſs Plin.* I feel the blood of the Plinlimmons riſe within me.

*Mr. Faſh.* I ſhould not be ſurpriſed, if under the idea of your being an ideot, he ſhould confine
you

you in fome old caftle in Ireland, without allowing you pen, ink or paper, to write to your friend, Mifs Bluehofe; without having the pleafure of being magnetifed; and without ever having the gratification of dining upon Hebrew roots.

*Mifs Plin.* I renounce him from this moment! With this breath *(blows through her fingers)* I blow away all my love! Imagine you fee it floating through the air, never to return to Lord Melcourt again!

*Mr. Fafh.* Methinks I behold the fairy chariot bearing away your affections! Oh! that I could arreft the richly freighted vehicle, and feize the invaluable prize.

*Mifs Plin.* Indeed? Are you in earneft?

*Mr. Fafh.* I am, upon my honour!

*Mifs Plin.* Ah! but you are fo wild, and you love all the women!

*Mr. Fafh.* I am like other young men, when under no particular engagement; like a bird in the grove, I wing from bough to bough; but once married, I fhould be as domeftic and as conftant as the turtle-dove.

*Mifs Plin.* If it be fo, I could be almoft induced---

*Mr, Fafh.* Come, come, let me feize this coy hand---fhew you have a fpirit to reward as well as to refent.

*Mifs Plin.* *(laughing)* It would be a good trick to play the Irifh peer.

*Mr. Fafh.* The ftudy of my life would be your happinefs.

*Mifs Plin.* Are you a gentleman?

*Mr. Fafh.* That you know by my name---and in point of character, I am totally different from Lord Melcourt---I love you paffionately.

*Mifs Plin.* That is no unpleafing intelligence.

*Mr. Fafh.* I do not walk in my fleep.

*Mife Plin.* I am very glad to hear that.

*Mr.*

*Mr. Faſh.* But no time is to be loſt---this li-
cenſe of Lord Melcourt's, with a ſmall change,
will ſerve our purpoſe.

*Miſs Plin.* Taffey will ſow us together in a
twinkle.

*Mr. Faſh.* Let us fly to the parſon.

(*Exeunt.*

Scene---*Another Apartment.*

*Enter Sir* Pepper Plinlimmon.

Well, if what I am informed of ſhould prove
true, that my girl has no inclination to Lord Melcourt, I ſhall not force her.

*Lady Plin.* (*behind the ſcenes*) Where is Sir
Pepper? Where is Sir Pepper?

*Sir P. Plin.* I hear Lady Plinlimmon's voice---
now ſhe is coming to pour upon me, as from a wide
mortar-piece.

*Enter Lady* Plinlimmon.

*Lady Plin.* Do you call me a wide mortar-piece,
Sir Pepper?---But let that paſs---I come to demand your authority over this wayward girl of
our's, who pretends to diſlike Lord Melcourt, becauſe he is not, forſooth, ſentimentally in love with
her.

*Sir P. Plin.* Without mutual affection, there is
no living together.

*Lady Plin.* Have we not lived theſe fifteen years
together.

*Sir P. Plin.* Yes! and how have we lived?

(*Enter*

*Enter Lady* BELLAIR.

*Lady Plin.* I have been gently expoſtulating with Sir Pepper, on his concurring with Iſabella's whim-ſical objection to Lord Melcourt.

*Lady B.* I-confeſs I ſide with Sir Pepper.

*Lady Plin.* Is it poſſible!

*Lady B.* Though the loſs is my brother's, I ſhall not offer a word to reconcile Sir Pepper to an engagement that does not meet with his daugh-ter's approbation.

*Lady Plin.* I am aſtoniſhed to hear Lady Bellair encourage a ruſtic notion that is unknown to the regions of faſhion.

*Lady B.* Your Ladyſhip muſt allow that mutual happineſs is the end propoſed. 'Tis the mark, which if the bride and bridegroom in the higher ſphere do not hit, it is becauſe they take a falſe aim.

*Lady Plin.* Morality, too!

*Lady B.* Am not I an inſtance of the folly of hurrying into an unavoidable engagement?

*Lady Plin.* Not in the leaſt. Does not the world encircle you with all its attractions? Do you not enjoy the advantages of wedlock, without the incumbrances?---your Lord's title, and a hand-ſome allowance?

*Lady B.* Your Ladyſhip forgets that Sir Pepper is preſent.

*Sir P. Plin.* I beg ſhe may not be interrupted on my account.

*Lady Plin.* Give me leave to aſk in what man-ner your Ladyſhip can be ſuppoſed to be a ſuf-ferer from your being ſeparated from Lord Bellair? Do your jewels ſhine leſs bright? Is the oſtrich-feather on your cap leſs playful? Is the lace---

*Sir P. Plin.* Zounds! Lady Plinlimmon, your
head

head is like a newfpaper after a birth-day---full of
nothing but gauzes, foils, and trimmings!

*Lady Plin.* Well, I ftand corrected. I give up
the point concerning my daughter, fince I find
every body is againft me,


Enter *Lord* MELCOURT.


*Lord Mel.* I am happy to find Lady Plinlimmon here; I am impatient to make this open de-
claration to her, that the concern I feel in not being
allowed to expect the honour of her alliance, is loft
in the higher confideration of Mifs Plinlimmon's
happinefs.

*Lady Plin.* Indeed, my Lord, you are too good,
to give way to the abfurd objections of an ignorant
girl.


Enter *Mr.* FASHION, *and Mifs* PLINLIMMON, *Mr.*
PHRENSY, *and Mr.* FANCY.


*Mr.* FASHION *and Mifs* PLINLIMMON, *kneel.*


*Mifs Plin.* Dear papa, give me and my hufband
your bleffing.

*Sir P. Plin.* Your hufband?

*Lady Plin.* Your hufband?

*Mr. Phrenfy.* 'Tis even fo. I had the honour
of giving her away.

*Lady Plin.* What do you fay to this, Lord Melcourt? (*To Mr.* FASHION) Audacious wretch, to
fteal my daughter.

*Lord Mel.* I can affure your Ladyfhip, Fafhion
is one of the moft ancient families in the kingdom, and has a title in obeyance.

*Lady Plin.* Well, if he has a title in obeyance.

*Sir*

*Sir P. Plin.* But will Lord Melcourt vouch for his character?

*Lord Mel.* Her Ladyſhip looks to the gaudy diſtinction of title; you, ſir, look for ſomething more ſubſtantial! Then let me tell you that Faſhion poſſeſſes thoſe titles which virtue's patent only can beſtow, honor and integrity.

*Sir P. Plin.* Then I am ſatisfied, come Lady Plinlimmon, let us forgive our child, (*Going up to Mr.* FASHION *and Lady* PLINLIMMON.

*Mr. Phrenſy.* But who is to reward me for my epithalamium? To whom ſhall I conſign it?

*Lord Mel.* I will tell you---conſign it to the fire-grate, that is the only way to inſure it a warm reception.

*Mr. Phrenſy.* Your envy at my talents prompts you to uſe ſo pitiful a conceit.

*Lord Mel.* Well, Phrenſy, I will indulge another conceit which will not offend you ſo much, and that is; I hope as long as you chooſe to be dead, you will live at Melcourt Hall.

*Mr. Phrenſy.* Egad, Melcourt Hall is ſo delightful a ſepulchre, I do not believe I ſhall ever wiſh to be alive again.

*Lord Mel.* Do you, then, never intend to return to life.

*Mr. Phrenſy.* Yes, I do, as ſoon as I have, by means of my ſubſcription) completed my poetical loan; my return to life will be a kind of an ovation: the triumphal proceſſion ſhall begin with my odes, each on his fiery Pegaſus; my ſatires, like tomahawks, ſhall next appear; then my elegies ſhall move like a weeping train of female captives, to theſe ſhall ſucceed my epigrams, a briſk troop of archers, with their pointed darts; my grand epic like a large unwieldy elephant, ſhall march by itſelf: then my tragedies, attired as widows, ſhall walk on one ſide, while my gaily veſted comedies ſhall trip on the other.

*Mr.*

, *Mr. Fancy.* And a mufical band of catcalls fhall walk between. ,

*Mr. Phrenfy.* Bafe canvafs dauber! how dare you interrupt me? when the poet's eye was in a fine Phrenfy rolling, when the mufe was kindling with conception! vile brufh-holder; you do not know the mifchief you have done; you have made the mufe mifcarry; the bright vifion is loft for ever--- (*Exit Mr.* PHRENSY.

*Lady B.* (*Advancing*) Now Phrenfy has finifhed his poetical rhapfody,-I beg I may prefent my congratulations to the bride and bridegroom; I muft confefs to you, Mr. Fafhion, that I little thought the gay irregular comedy of your bachelor life would have terminated with fo abrupt and moral a conclufion; as for you, my dear, though I am not to call you fifter, you will always be the object of my tender folicitude.

*Mifs. Plin.* I am a giddy creature, but I hope I fhall never forfeit your protection, I fhall leave to others to purfue the varying modes and fopperies of the day; this is the Fafhion (*pointing to Fafhion*) that I fhall adopt, and to this Fafhion I fhall be ever conftant.

*Lord Mel.* Bravo! Matrimony infpires you, well as it is now, my turn to fpeak, I beg you will both accept of my beft wifhes; may happinefs lead you through life, along her moft fmooth and flowry path.

*Mifs Plin.* Well, my lord, fince you take my tricking you in fuch perfect good humour, when I am miftrefs of my fortune, I will lend you whatever money you ftand in need of.

*Mr. Fafh.* (*difpleafed*) Lord Melcourt does not want our money, I prefume.

*Mifs. Plin.* I hope to fee your Lordfhip at our houfe in the country; I fuppofe, Mr. Fafhion, you have one fomewhere.

*Lord* ,

*Lord Mel.* Fashion's country house, I am afraid, is little better than a castle in the air, but till he has one erected upon a more solid foundation, I entreat Mr. and Mrs. Fashion will look upon Melcourt Hall as their own.

*Miss Plin.* Egad this is handsome: I have one thing more to recommend to your Lordship.

*Lord Mel.* What are your commands?

*Miss Plin.* (*half aside*) Be sure you never mention the crooked legs.

*Lord Mel.* Depend upon my discretion---come, let us all pass some chearful days under this roof; let reproaches and complainings cease, let good humour, social intercourse, pleasantry and content succeed.

END OF THE COMEDY.

EPILOGUE.

# EPILOGUE

BY THE RIGHT HON. FIELD MARSHAL CONWAY.

*Spoken by Miſs Farren.*

---

*WITH gloomy bodings for his bantling play,
Our Author came to me the other day,
A boon to aſk, tho' half afraid to break it;
He'd got an Epilogue, and I muſt ſpeak it.---
All means he fain would try, if not too late,
Still to avert his dread, impending fate.
Sad viſions, too, diſtract his anxious brain;
Rumours of ills, that wait the ſcribbling train.
'Tis ſaid your taſte for Comedy is flown;
That darling child you once were proud to own:
That Shakeſpear's fires no more your ſenſes rouze;
Congreve and Vanbrugh ſeldom fill the houſe;
While childiſh pageants ſtuff the crouded ſcene,
No mortal even gueſſing what they mean;
Fierce wars they wage, and dreadful battles try,
With bloodleſs conflict: all one knows not why.
Till by the friendly banners we are told,
There Macedon's, there Perſia's chief behold!
Juſt as on ſigns th' informing words declare,
This the Red Lion; that is the Black Bear.
Queens, and their maids of honor, wait in vain.
Till their mute lovers ſhall their ſuit explain.
They'd often heard, indeed from Greece and Rome,

That

That love was blind; but ne'er that he was dumb.
There too thofe motly, female, manly graces,
With almoft all things naked, but their faces;
Thofe modern Picts, at whom we gaze with wonder;
While their keen falchions cut whole ranks afunder.
Great Rufty-fufti's triumphs thus we greet ;
Six holy Roman emp'rors breathlefs at her feet.
Nor lefs the neighb'ring temples of Apollo,
With equal fteps the bright example follow.
There beardlefs warriors fqueak each other's doom ;
And filken Vandals plan the fall of Rome.
There demigods by entrechâts advance,
And Carthage flames demolifh'd in a dance.
Arms clafh, loud thunders roar, and chariots rattle ;
While jarring trumpets animate the battle.

    Now critics, if you're angry think on thefe,
And fpare the bard who ftrives at leaft to pleafe:
Judge, and be judg'd, in anger juft, I pray :
*Audire alteram partem* is fair play.
In fuch a caufe, altho' the tafk be hard ;
I'll be myfelf of counfel for our bard ;
I've fuch authorities as none refufes,
Fleta's, and Coke's, and Blackftone's of the Mufes ;
Farqhuar and Rowe, and Wycherly we boaft !
And Avon's mighty feer, himfelf a hoft !

    Yet, for I feel my female fears increafe,
Tho' arm'd for war, *yet ftill I wifh* for peace:
We own your pow'r, confefs your wond'rous fway,
Whom all our great dramatic realms obey:

                         No

No merit we can claim, till you befriend it,
Wit is not wit, unless your taste commend it :
From th' Author's anvil a mere sluggish mass ;
Your plaudits stamp the coin, and bid it pass.
By your mild sentence then decide our fate :
Far better to be good than to be great !
Like Britain's Monarch, act your generous parts,
And fix your empire, in our greatful hearts.

## FINIS.

www.ingramcontent.com/pod-product-compliance
Lightning Source LLC
Chambersburg PA
CBHW032354020726
47499CB00008B/2736